PRAISE

DISCOURSE ON JUSTIFICATION

"As an evangelical theologian who teaches and writes on Roman Catholic theology and practice, I get many questions from evangelicals about their Catholic family members and friends: Are Catholics Christians? Isn't Roman Catholicism a works-based religion? If Roman Catholicism has an improper understanding of the doctrine of justification—'not only the remission of sins but also the sanctification and renewal of the interior person'—can Catholics be justified, declared not guilty but righteous instead? This new, highly readable production of Richard Hooker's book on justification helps us answer those questions in ways that may be surprising!"

—*Dr. Gregg R. Allison, Professor of Christian Theology at Southern Baptist Theological Seminary; Secretary of the Evangelical Theological Society; author of* Roman Catholic Theology and Practice: An Evangelical Assessment *(with Chris Castaldo) and* The Unfinished Reformation: What Unites and Divides Catholics and Protestants after 500 Years.

"Happy, secure Protestants recognize that we won't do ourselves, or our spiritual progeny, long-term good by caricaturing Catholicism. There are problems, yes. Significant problems. The Reformation is not over. Good fences remain. And we will do better to love across such boundaries in the name of Jesus than to pretend they don't matter. But there's no virtue in distorting truth by exaggerating errors, or losing our capacity to give a holy benefit of the doubt. If we

Protestants love the truth, and not just our tradition (ironically), we might give Hooker the hearing he deserves—and help keep young Protestants from future surprises."

—*David Mathis, Senior Teacher and Executive Editor at desiringGod.org; Pastor at Cities Church, Saint Paul, MN; author of* Habits of Grace.

"Brad Littlejohn and his associates have once again provided an accessible yet loyal version of a work of Richard Hooker that should still be known and valued, and that in a theological world wider than Anglicanism. In this extended and 'learned' sermon, Hooker shows that a clear loyalty to the Protestant principle of justification by faith does not necessarily deny salvation to those who erroneously deny the principle. We can and should carefully and accurately assert what we understand to be basic Christian theology and yet understand that those who disagree are not thereby cut off from the salvation that is the essence of the Christian Gospel. And we can delight in the learned rhetorical expression of this unity in diversity."

—*Rev. Canon W. David Neelands, Dean Emeritus of Divinity at Trinity College, University of Toronto.*

"*A Learned Discourse on Justification in Modern English* is a treasure for the church. Hooker's original work is supremely important. It further develops the question, 'What is Anglican doctrine?' For many, Hooker is the Theologian of Anglicanism. In this modern English version, the editors have made this sixteenth-century work accessible and readable for the modern mind. Read this work and be anchored in the article by which the church stands or falls."

—*Bishop Julian Dobbs, Anglican Diocese of the Living Word (ACNA).*

"It is a tremendous service to the church to have this excellent modern edition of Richard Hooker's bold and nuanced defense of the Reformed doctrine of justification by faith alone against the heresies and corruptions of Rome. As he beautifully puts it, Christ alone has satisfied and appeased God's wrath, not our blood or our best works, and He is 'the only garment which, once worn, covers the shame of our defiled natures, hides the imperfections of our works, and preserves us blameless in God's sight.' It is an immense joy to read this exposition from a great Anglican theologian."

—*Rev. Dr. Lee Gatiss, Director of Church Society, Editor of* The First Book of Homilies: The Church of England's Official Sermons in Modern English.

"This volume finally offers contemporary readers an expertly rendered text of what is rightly called 'one of the classic statements of Reformational soteriology.' Hooker's *Discourse on Justification*, here wonderfully presented in modernized English and equipped with a splendid explanatory introduction by Brad Littlejohn, is a crystalline presentation of a central Christian doctrine that has divided Christians for centuries, even as the doctrine's proper understanding has faded in recent decades. Hooker's penetrating, measured, faithful, and charitable exposition proves to be a powerful medicine for modern confusions and dogmatic apathy. The editors' accessible edition represents an act of theological generosity of the highest order and deserves to be widely studied."

—*Dr. Ephraim Radner, Professor of Historical Theology, Wycliffe College at the University of Toronto.*

A Learned Discourse on

Justification

A LEARNED DISCOURSE OF JUSTIFICATION, WORKS, AND HOW THE FOUNDATION OF FAITH IS OVERTHROWN IN MODERN ENGLISH

by Richard Hooker

Edited by Bradford Littlejohn, Rhys Laverty, and Ken Cook

Copyright © 2022 The Davenant Institute

All rights reserved.

ISBN: 1-949716-10-4

ISBN-13: 978-1-949716-10-8

Front cover image is "Gold Cross in the Interior of a Church in the Lake District, Cumbria, UK." Photo taken by David Forster.

Cover design by Rachel Rosales, Orange Peal Design

Typeset and proofread by Mikael Good

TABLE OF CONTENTS

Introduction *Bradford Littlejohn*	iv
Editorial Approach	xxv
I: The Real Disagreement Between Rome and Protestantism	1
II: Could Our Fathers Be Saved?	16
III: What Is the Foundation of Faith?	32
IV: Can the Elect Deny the Foundation of Faith?	39
V: Does Rome Directly Deny the Foundation of Faith?	51
VI: Conclusion	74

INTRODUCTION

Bradford Littlejohn

The Article by Which the Church Stands or Falls?

EVEN today, when catechesis isn't what it once was, nearly every Protestant knows that the defining doctrine of Protestantism is *justification by faith alone*. Martin Luther went so far as to call this "the article by which the church stands or falls." Protestants believe in salvation by faith, Catholics in salvation by works. Simple, right?

Anyone who has spent much time reading about the sixteenth-century Reformation, or indeed talking to a contemporary Roman Catholic, knows that it is not that simple. Protestants, after all, have always contended that while salvation may rest on faith alone, this must be a faith that never *remains alone*—saving faith is always accompanied by good works. Authentic Protestant theology is not antinomianism, whatever Catholic critics or libertine modern evangelicals might think. And authentic Roman Catholic theology is not works-righteousness, whatever Protestant critics or untutored Catholic laypeople might imagine. Just as the Protestant doctrine of justification has always been nuanced, so has the Roman—especially after more open engagement with Protestant theology in the later twentieth century.

This nuance raises a troubling question. If the doctrine of justification by faith is not so simple after all, then how can we insist on it as the pillar on which the church stands or falls? What do we say about the little old lady who's been a devout churchgoer her entire life, but cannot articulate the niceties of this doctrine? Is the authenticity of her faith in question? Against any such over-intellectualizing of Christian faith, we must take a firm stand. We are justified by faith in *Christ* alone, not by faith in the doctrine of justification by faith alone. If the proper formulation of *sola fide* replaces Christ Himself, and His death on our behalf, as the object of our faith, we have replaced a Pelagianism of bodily works-righteousness with a Pelagianism of mental works-righteousness.

If insisting too rigidly on the right understanding of justification is one pitfall, though, there is clearly another: neglecting the importance of the doctrine all together. This pitfall is probably more widespread in the contemporary church. Lulled by centuries of pietism into thinking that all that matters is being well-intentioned and having the right feelings, we might be prone to ask why debates over justification should matter at all. If all of us love Jesus, all of us have faith, and all of us try to do good works, why should it matter if we can't agree on how exactly to parse the relationship of faith and works, Christ and ourselves?

Against the errors of both such doctrinal maximalism and doctrinal minimalism, Richard Hooker's *Learned Discourse on Justification, Works, and How the Foundation of Faith is Overthrown*, first preached in 1586 and later published in 1612, offers a powerful antidote. Nearly 450 years on, it remains one of *the* classic statements of Reformational soteriology, presenting a lucid and precise account of what

INTRODUCTION

Protestants do and do not believe about the doctrine of justification, along with a careful summary of what their Catholic opponents held. Readers seeking a helmsman who can faithfully guide them through the fog that so often bedevils this crucial conversation need look no further.

However, as the second part of its original title suggests, the *Learned Discourse* is about more than just justification. Rather, it seeks to answer a much more fundamental set of questions: how do we make sense of doctrinal difference? How do we take doctrinal error seriously without damning to hell everyone who might disagree with us? Is it possible to be wrong—even about a central doctrine—and still be saved? Hooker's attempt to parse these timeless questions, using the doctrine of justification as a case study, is (despite being centuries old) a breath of fresh air in an era dominated by persistent woolly-headedness masquerading as Christian love. It is possible, it turns out, to celebrate God's mercy to erring sinners without denying that bad ideas have bad consequences. Even if Catholics and Protestants should one day resolve their differences on justification, this larger aim of Hooker's work will retain its relevance and usefulness as long as the church endures.

It is perhaps all the more remarkable that a work of such power and enduring impact should have appeared almost by accident. Certainly, Hooker never set out to write a treatise on justification. The discourse, as we have it today, is the product of three sermons preached on successive Sundays at the Temple Church in London in early 1586—the response to an audacious and unexpected challenge from Hooker's junior associate, Walter Travers. Before telling that story, however, perhaps we should take a step back and ask, "Who was Richard Hooker?"

Hooker and the Church of England in the Age of Elizabeth

Richard Hooker (c. 1554–1600) is a name little known today outside of the Anglican tradition, and less and less even within it. His works, once standard reading for any educated Englishman, have receded far into our cultural rearview mirror, increasingly unreadable and seemingly obsolete in our postmodern age. But they are, as I hope you will find, nearly as relevant today as when they were first penned, and as worthy of our attention as the other literary monuments of the Elizabethan Golden Age.[1]

Hooker wrote in the 1580s and 1590s, that high tide of Elizabethan intellectual and literary culture which defined the shape of our language and culture right down to the present. While Hooker was writing his *magnum opus*, the *Lawes of Ecclesiasticall Politie*,[2] Shakespeare was just on the opposite bank of the Thames writing *The Taming of the Shrew*, and Spenser had just returned to Ireland after coming to London to publish and promote his *Faerie Queene*. Francis Bacon was a leading advisor at court, just beginning his literary career. As with these other men, the scale of Hooker's achievement looms up out of the relative mediocrity of his predecessors with a suddenness that can baffle the historian. Stanley Archer observes, "It is no more possible to account

---

[1] For a fuller introduction to Hooker's life and thought, see my *Richard Hooker: A Companion to His Life and Work* (Eugene, OR: Cascade Books, 2016).

[2] See W. Bradford Littlejohn, Bradley Belschner, and Brian Marr, eds., *The Laws of Ecclesiastical Polity in Modern English*, vol. 1: *Preface– Book IV* (Moscow, ID: The Davenant Press, 2018).

INTRODUCTION

for Hooker's achievement than for those of Shakespeare and Milton, Spenser and Bacon."[3]

Indeed, though merely a quiet and unassuming scholar rather than a visionary church leader like Luther or Calvin, Hooker deserves mentioning in their company for the clarity and timeliness of his theological vision, without whose insights Protestant theology would be forever impoverished. Of course, although Hooker left a legacy from which all Protestants can profit, he is particularly known as the theologian of Anglicanism. But Hooker would have been surprised to hear that there was any such "ism"; even in his *Laws*, he wrote in defense of the Church of England, as it had been established in the reign of Queen Elizabeth I, which he took to be a particular national branch of the Reformed churches. In his earlier works, like the *Learned Discourse*, even this specificity is lacking; Hooker sees himself as standing within a broad international Reformed Protestantism, caught off guard by any suggestion that he might be saying anything particularly new or controversial. By the 1580s, however, nearly everything in English theology was liable to be the subject of controversy, as a group of dissidents now known as "Puritans" leveled charges that the Church of England was "but halfly reformed."

And to be sure, the checkered history of the early Church of England left plenty of loose ends in its reformation for the more zealous to complain about. Beginning with Henry VIII's fitful and inconstant reformation, prompted more by dynastic and fiscal concerns than by theological convictions, the Church of England lurched, in just a fifteen-year period, through at least four distinct phases.

---

[3] *Richard Hooker* (Boston: Twayne, 1983), 1.

In 1546 it was autonomous from Rome but still traditionalist Catholic in its doctrine and practice. It then witnessed first a thoroughgoing embrace of Reformed theology and rapid reformation of worship under Edward VI, then a violent Roman Catholic counter-reformation under Queen Mary, and finally Elizabeth I's imposition of a moderate Protestantism that owed much to Melanchthonian Lutheranism, but which soon provoked a Puritan backlash.

Richard Hooker was born in the bloodiest and most tumultuous phase of this whole bloody and tumultuous story, sometime in late 1553 or early 1554 in Heavitree, a village on the outskirts of Exeter in southwest England, which was then, as now, a prosperous port and a cathedral city. Hooker's family was not particularly prosperous, save for his uncle John, who was not merely well-to-do but well-educated and well-connected, most notably to the great Italian reformer Peter Martyr Vermigli, who had been serving as Professor of Divinity at Oxford under the Protestant King Edward VI. The year 1554, however, was not a very good time to have such connections. Queen Mary (known to history not unreasonably as "Bloody Mary" for her martyrdom of hundreds of Protestants) had just ascended the throne on the boy-king's death, and was determined to reverse the rapid progress the Reformation had made in England over the past few years. Vermigli had fled to the continent, along with many of his friends and students, including John Hooker and Vermigli's star student, John Jewel, who was also to play a significant role in the young Richard's life. Those Protestants who already held high office in the Church of England were not so fortunate; they remained at their posts, were arrested, and before long burned at the stake: most notable among them were Bishop

INTRODUCTION

John Hooper on February 9, 1555, Bishops Nicholas Ridley and Hugh Latimer on October 16 of that year, and Archbishop Thomas Cranmer on March 21 of the following year.

Fortunately for the Hooker family, the Protestant cause did not have to wait long for a dramatic change of fortunes. The sudden death of Mary in late 1558 and accession of the firmly Protestant Queen Elizabeth struck contemporary Protestants as a great act of divine deliverance; Hooker was to write of her nearly four decades later as "God's most happy instrument by him miraculously kept for works of so miraculous preservation and safety to others."[4]

Elizabeth's accession brought the exiled English Protestants hastening home, but the delicate work of hammering out a contested "middle way" was just beginning. In the early years of the Elizabethan Settlement, all of Elizabeth's bishops expected further reformation to move forward in due course, once the dust had settled from the chaos of the recent violent transitions. Elizabeth herself, however, seems to have genuinely favored a more ceremonial mode of worship, and feared the religious radicalism that she attributed to the two-hour long sermons favored by more zealous Reformers. Besides, the maintenance of some outward trappings of the old medieval religion (whether it be the threefold order of bishops, priests, and deacons; the special vestments worn by priests while celebrating the liturgy; or the retention of ceremonies like confirmation) was, Eliz-

---

[4] *The Laws of Ecclesiastical Polity*, Book V, Dedication, para. 10. Spelling and punctuation modernized. Full text available at: https://oll.libertyfund.org/title/keble-the-works-of-richard-hooker-vol-2.

abeth realized, politically desirable. After all, the mere accession of a Protestant monarch had hardly converted the whole kingdom to the new Reformed faith; many thousands of closet Catholics, some among the high nobility, remained throughout the realm, their loyalty to the new regime uncertain. By retaining many forms of worship familiar to them, Elizabeth deemed, she could make their outward conformity easier and reduce the risk of rebellions or conspiracies—ever-present threats throughout her long reign. Just as importantly, she could ease the alarm of Catholic monarchs abroad, especially King Philip II of Spain, who was on the lookout for any opportunity to reassert control of an island kingdom he had briefly gained through his marriage to the short-lived Queen Mary. Spanish diplomats could be selectively shown the more traditionalist worship of the cathedrals and royal court and left with the impression that perhaps England wasn't too Protestant after all.

Unfortunately for Elizabeth, some of her more zealous subjects could be left with that impression as well. Beginning with an outbreak of controversy over the required clerical vestments in 1564–66 (the so-called Vestiarian Controversy), Elizabeth and her bishops found themselves facing a series of reformist agitations, each seemingly more comprehensive and uncompromising than the last. The bishops, though sympathetic to the protests, insisted that there was nothing genuinely sub-Protestant about the debated ceremonies, which ultimately concerned matters of *adiaphora* or "things indifferent," practices on which Scripture was silent and concern for edification of the body should guide us.[5] From the standpoint of most of the

---

[5] For an excellent discussion see ch. 5 of W. J. Torrance Kirby, *The Zurich Connection and Tudor Political Theology* (Leiden: Brill, 2007).

church's leaders, what mattered above all was the fact, which none then denied, that when it came to doctrine at least, the Church of England was firmly in step with the Reformed consensus abroad.

Increasingly, however, as tension heightened between the bishops and "the hotter sort of Protestants," as the early Puritans were then sometimes called, the controversy tended to expand beyond mere matters of ritual. More radical leaders such as Thomas Cartwright and Walter Travers, drawing inspiration from Geneva and other continental churches, began to call for an overhaul of the whole system of church government along broadly presbyterian lines. As the stakes were raised, so was the rhetoric. Some Puritans began to insist, in terms perhaps familiar enough to us today but out-of-step with the early Protestant Reformers, that the Bible was the only standard for liturgy and church government, and any church that failed to radically reform itself in conformity to Scripture alone was not worthy of the name of church. In such an atmosphere, conformist leaders began to see Puritans as on the road toward Anabaptist schism, while the Puritans, for their part, condemned the establishment, clad as it was in the "rags of popery," for being too soft on Rome.

It was against this increasingly tense background that the young Richard had pursued his theological education. John Hooker had found his nephew to be a boy of precocious talents, and funded his education at the local grammar school. By 1568 or 1569, Richard was deemed ready for further study at university, a privilege reserved for just a handful in his day. To financially support Richard's studies, John Hooker turned to his old friend John Jewel, now installed as bishop of nearby Salisbury and the leading apologist of the Church of England. Jewel interviewed Richard, was deeply impressed by his talents, and agreed to secure him a place at his own *alma mater*, Corpus Christi College at Oxford, provide financial support, and keep an eye on Richard's developing career.

Hooker excelled at Oxford, rising by 1579 to become a fellow of Corpus Christi, and earned the lifelong friendship of influential individuals in the Elizabethan Church. These included his older mentor John Rainolds (an important spokesman for the moderate Puritan movement in the decades to come) and his students Edwin Sandys (son of the Archbishop of York, and later a leading member of Parliament) and George Cranmer (a relation of the late Archbishop Cranmer). As best we can tell, at this stage the younger Hooker was initially sympathetic to many of the concerns of the Puritan party, though perhaps not their more radical wing.

By the time the 1580s began, Hooker was being encouraged by his mentors to take a more active part in church affairs. He was ordained a deacon in 1579 and a priest in 1581, and shortly afterward was given an opportunity to preach at Paul's Cross, the great public pulpit by St. Paul's Cathedral where aspiring preachers could expect to have many of the great men and women of London, including sometimes the Queen herself, among their audience. Never one to make things too easy for himself, he chose as his topic the doctrine of predestination, offering, as it would appear from the accounts we have, a moderate version of the doctrine that was closer to that taught by Heinrich Bullinger of Zurich than to Calvin and Beza's stronger doctrine,

INTRODUCTION

which was then coming increasingly into vogue.[6] Predestination and controversy have always gone hand-in-hand, and Hooker quickly encountered his fair share of detractors, although, since John Aylmer, Bishop of London, appears to have supported him, it turned out well enough for him in the end. During this first stay in London, Hooker also appears to have perhaps first made the acquaintance of John Churchman, who was to serve as a landlord, patron, and eventually father-in-law in the coming years.

A little over three years later, in early 1585, Hooker's well-positioned friends secured for him the nomination to the prestigious position of Master of the Temple. The Temple Church, so named because it had been founded by the Knights Templar in the late twelfth century, and built as a small-scale replica of the Church of the Holy Sepulchre in Jerusalem, served as the parish of the lawyers and law students of the Inner and Middle Temple. As the heart of the legal profession in England, the Temple was a position of substantial influence and political importance, and Hooker's appointment to such a position at the age of just thirty-one tells us something about how well he had impressed his superiors. However, there was also a fair bit of political wrangling that lay behind the decision.

After several years of relative quiet, the presbyterian movement had burst back onto the scene in the early 1580s. John Whitgift, once appointed Archbishop of Canterbury in 1583, moved quickly to enforce strict conformity on the Church of England, as Elizabeth seems to have intended in

---

[6] See David Neelands, "Richard Hooker's Paul's Cross Sermon," in *Paul's Cross and the Culture of Persuasion in England, 1520–1640*, ed. W. J. Torrance Kirby and P. G. Stanwood (Leiden: Brill, 2013), 245–61.

selecting him for the position. By requiring Puritan-minded ministers to subscribe unreservedly to the Thirty-Nine Articles and Book of Common Prayer, he hoped to weed out conscientious objectors. Instead, he provoked a backlash. Beleaguered ministers quickly appealed to sympathetic noblemen to push for reforms in Parliament, and in the meantime gravitated toward the more radical presbyterian wing, seeing a complete overhaul of the Church of England as the only way to attain their aims. By 1584, a secret presbyterian network was taking shape throughout the country, and it would grow and consolidate over the next five years.

Walter Travers, one of the leading presbyterian theorists, who had not even been ordained in the Church of England, had enough powerful friends to secure a position as Reader (i.e., assistant minister) in the Temple Church back in 1581, and with the retirement of the aged Master, was expected to succeed him. However, in the increasingly polarized climate, Whitgift and Aylmer intervened to select a more suitable candidate. Travers had already succeeded in swaying many of the members of the Temple to a puritan and even presbyterian perspective, so Hooker was selected as a middle-of-the-road candidate who would hopefully be acceptable to the parishioners, and to Travers, but reliable from the standpoint of the authorities.

Conflict began almost immediately, however. Travers had already gone some ways towards reorganizing the church along quasi-presbyterian lines, and he asked Hooker to wait for the congregation to formally approve his appointment to the post before taking up his ministry (since, for Travers, congregational approval was essential for a legitimate ministerial call). Hooker was bewildered by such a violation of protocol, and declined. After this inauspicious

INTRODUCTION

start, Travers treated Hooker's ministry with suspicion, never really conceding the authority of this government appointee five years his junior.

So it was not long before the tension exploded into a public confrontation. In early 1586, Hooker made an offhand remark toward the end of one of his sermons about the medieval ancestors who lived before the light of reformation dawned: "God, I doubt not, was merciful to save thousands of them, though they lived in popish superstitions, inasmuch as they sinned ignorantly; but the truth is now laid open before our eyes." To Travers, already primed to look for any sign of softness toward Rome, this was proof that all his fears about Hooker had been justified. Rather than conferring with Hooker to see if he had understood him, Travers, deeming "the hope of the fruit of our communication being small, upon experience of former conferences,"[7] decided to take Hooker to task publicly in his own afternoon sermon. Hooker, for his part, decided the issue was important enough to warrant an extended clarification, and undertook, over the next three Sundays, to unfold in some detail the doctrine of justification by faith, the precise nature of the Roman error, and how it might be that even those infected with this error could yet have been saved. Travers, increasingly agitated, used his afternoon preaching slot to denounce Hooker more and more forcefully. As word got out, the spectacle of this preaching war drew crowds to the Temple Church, and soon the authorities were alarmed.

---

[7] Travers, *A Supplication to the Privy Counsel*, in *The Folger Library Edition of the Works of Richard Hooker*, ed. Laetitia Yeandle, vol. 5: *Tractates and Sermons* (Cambridge, MA: The Belknap Press of Harvard University Press, 1990), 202 (spelling modernized).

Archbishop Whitgift, hearing of the proceedings, issued an order silencing Travers, upon which Travers appealed his case to the Queen's Privy Council, denouncing Hooker for various breaches of orthodoxy and alleging that "the like...have not been heard in public places, within this land, since Queen Mary's days."[8] Hooker, for his part, responded by defending his orthodoxy and expressing frustration over Travers's high-handed refusal to follow the appropriate channels for expressing his concern; the canons of the Church of England stipulated that if any preacher be suspected of dangerous or unorthodox teaching, the concerned party should bring the matter to the attention of the bishop, instead of airing the matter publicly. Whatever the ins and outs of the theological debate, Travers's breach of protocol was undeniable, and the Council summarily dismissed Travers from his post. Hooker, however, found his position at the Temple quite uncomfortable thereafter, with many of his parishioners sympathetic to their banished Reader, and he eagerly accepted transfer to a less prestigious rural parish in 1591.

The Enduring Relevance of the *Discourse*

Unpleasant though the controversy may have been for the conflict-averse Hooker, it was not without its rich harvest of fruits for the church. An older generation of biographers was apt to claim that in the Temple controversy were sown the seeds of Hooker's masterpiece, *The Lawes of Ecclesiasticall Politie*, which Hooker chipped away at throughout the 1590s. This is now recognized as unlikely; after all, whereas the

---

[8] Travers, *Supplication*, 208 (spelling modernized).

INTRODUCTION

Lawes is concerned above all with the nature of biblical authority and church polity, the showdown with Travers revolved around soteriology (although differences over ecclesiology certainly lurked not far in the background). Even if Hooker had never gone on to write the *Lawes*, however, the masterpiece distilled from his sermonic defenses against Travers, *The Learned Discourse of Justification*, would rank as one of the enduring classics of Reformation theology.

It is one of the tragedies of post-Reformation confessionalization that more Protestants have not drunk deeply from this well of eloquence and theological insight. Having been pigeonholed as an "Anglican" theologian after the deep conflicts of the seventeenth century, Hooker is rarely read by Reformed or Lutheran churchmen, but the doctrine preached in the *Learned Discourse* speaks for all Protestants. It offers, indeed, perhaps as pithy a summary of the shared magisterial Protestant doctrine of justification by faith alone as you are likely to find in the whole of the sixteenth century.[9] Of course, this does not mean that contemporary evangelical readers may not find Hooker's treatment of the topic somewhat jarring. To those raised on the notion that Protestantism and Rome are as far apart as light and darkness, Hooker's statements that "[t]hey teach, as we do, that

---

[9] For good expositions of Hooker's doctrine of justification in the larger Reformation context, see Ranall Ingalls, "Sin and Grace," in *A Companion to Richard Hooker*, ed W. J. Torrance Kirby (Leiden: Brill, 2008), 151–83; and Luca Baschera, "Righteousness Imputed and Inherent: Hooker's Soteriology in the Context of 16th Century Continental Reformed Theology," in *Richard Hooker and Reformed Orthodoxy*, ed. W. Bradford Littlejohn and Scott N. Kindred-Barnes (Gottingen: Vandenhoeck and Ruprecht, 2017), 241–54.

God alone justifies the soul of man without any other cooperative cause of justice….They teach, as we do, that no one has ever attained justification but by the merits of Jesus Christ" are apt to surprise. Is he not being awfully soft on Rome?

Certainly this is what Travers thought, alleging that Hooker had "so set out the agreement of the church of Rome with us, and their disagreement from us, as if we had consented in the greatest and weightiest points, and differed only in certain smaller matters."[10] Succeeding generations of Anglican hagiography and historiography have sought to convert what Travers saw as vice into evidence of Hooker's preeminent Anglican virtue: peace, moderation, and sweet reasonableness. This perspective seems bolstered by the most quoted line of the *Discourse*: "I must confess: if it is an error to think that God may be merciful to save men even when they err, my greatest comfort is my error! If it were not for the love which I hold for this error, I would wish neither to speak nor to live!" Is not Hooker here trying to diminish the distance between Rome and the Reformation, insisting that Catholics, too, belong to the visible Church and can be saved? Well, yes and no.

There is no question that Hooker was, for his time, an unusually irenic theologian, one who possessed that rare gift of moral imagination—the ability to see a hotly disputed question from the other party's point of view. It is equally true that Hooker held a capacious understanding of the visible church, insisting that all of the baptized who had not openly apostatized should be considered in some sense members of the Church, even if only outwardly. The debate

---

[10] Travers, *Supplication*, 203, spelling modernized.

with Travers, however, concerned not the boundaries of the visible Church but the invisible: who might be saved in the eyes of God? Repeatedly over the course of his career, Hooker expressed his preference for reverent agnosticism on this subject: it is not ours to pry into the hearts of others, nor to lay down the bounds of God's mercy. Still, Hooker had no intention of making any radical departure from Reformation soteriology. He remained convinced that only those who clung to Christ as their only Savior could be saved. The question, then, was simply whether someone could so cling to Christ in faith without rightly understanding that faith. Hooker believed that for many of us, our hearts are sounder than our heads, and saving faith could exist even in the face of bad doctrine.

The logic of Hooker's argument, while couched in sometimes elusive language (which we have sought to render as accessible as possible in this edition), is really quite straightforward. There are two ways, he says, to deny a proposition: directly, or by logical consequence. I might, for instance, deny that there had ever been a Queen Elizabeth I; or else I might, slightly more plausibly, argue that the fourteenth-century Katherine Swynford had never been the mistress of John of Gaunt. Since, however, Katherine Swynford was in fact the great-great-great-great-grandmother of Elizabeth I, denying her union with John of Gaunt would, by logical consequence, entail that Elizabeth I had never been born. Or, to take a more subtle example that perhaps brings us a bit nearer to the logic of Hooker's argument, I might deny that Henry VII, the first Tudor king, had ever had any just title to the throne. If not, then neither did his granddaughter Elizabeth, and therefore, although I would not be denying her historical existence, I would, *by logical consequence* at least, be denying that she had ever truly been *Queen* Elizabeth.

To apply this to the matter at hand, Hooker is staunch in his insistence that the Protestant understanding of justification *sola fide* is not *itself* the foundation of faith, but rather the only full and consistent account of the foundation of faith: if you want to know what it means that "Christ alone is Savior," you will have to end up, eventually, at the Protestant position; anything else introduces (however subtly and implicitly) a form of human self-salvation. Therefore, argues Hooker, there is a world of difference between someone who says, "Jesus Christ did not come in the flesh" (cf. 1 John 4:2–3) and someone who says, "Jesus Christ alone saves us, through the infusion of a habitual righteousness which enables us to bring forth fruits of actual righteousness." The latter doctrine may ultimately undermine the foundations of faith, but it does so only by several intermediate steps of reasoning, which many Christians—even very smart ones—may fail to grasp. Various levels of heresy may be plotted on a spectrum, depending on just how directly or indirectly they contradict the central pillar of Christian faith, and we should not hesitate to extend a judgment of charity about the souls of those involved in more indirect forms of error.

Contra Travers, who had insisted that Hooker was here airing radical new ideas that all but capitulated to Rome—and contra later Anglican interpreters eager to portray Hooker as architect of a *via media* between Rome and Geneva—Richard Bauckham has persuasively argued that there was little fundamentally new about Hooker's argument here.[11] Plenty of Protestants, in England and outside of it, had argued that Rome was still in some sense a Christian church, and that not all within her pale were doomed to perdition—especially if we were speaking of those (as Hooker was) who lived before the greater light of the Reformation had dawned. Indeed, Hooker quotes from Reformed stalwarts such as Girolamo Zanchi in defense of his basic claims; it is perhaps no coincidence that when an English translation of Zanchi's work appeared a few years later from a Puritan press, it quietly omitted the passage that Hooker had quoted![12]

Still, some might fairly ask why Hooker is so keen on making these distinctions. Is not the effect, as Travers had charged, to minimize the differences between Protestantism and Rome, to lower the stakes and soothe erring souls with the false assurance that it didn't matter that much what they thought of justification? In voicing such worries, Travers speaks for many throughout Reformed history, and indeed many in the Reformed church today, who are quick to pounce on any attempt to nuance the lines of division between orthodoxy and error. Indeed, Travers takes particular aim at Hooker's use of scholastic logic-chopping rather than simple Bible preaching: isn't this just an attempt to make fuzzy what God's Word has made clear?

---

[11] Richard Bauckham, "Hooker, Travers, and the Church of Rome in the 1580s," *Journal of Ecclesiastical History* 29, no. 1 (January 1978): 37–50.

[12] See *H. Zanchius His Confession of Christian Religion* (Cambridge, John Legat, 1599), 56–57. An unabridged modern English translation can be found in *De Religione Christianae Fides (Confession of the Christian Religion)*, ed. Luca Baschera and Christian Moser, 2 vols. (Leiden: Brill, 2007).

Hooker would insist that this fundamentally misunderstands his purpose. Indeed, as Bauckham has shown, Hooker's original statement that so incensed Travers occurred in the context of a polemical sermon *against* Rome, and this basic purpose was never left behind. Throughout the 1570s and 1580s, Roman apologists had made considerable hay among Englishmen by a sentimental appeal to the state of their ancestors' souls. If Protestantism were true, they alleged, that meant that their English grandfathers and grandmothers were invariably burning in hell, lost as they were in the darkness of a pre-Reformation theology of justification. Such an argument had to be countered if Protestantism was to persuasively present itself as a renewal within the one Church, and not the sudden rebirth of a Church long extinct.

Moreover, Hooker realized that nothing was to be gained over the long run by exaggerating and caricaturing Rome's errors. What Travers (and many Anglicans since) saw as an overt attempt by Hooker to go "soft on Rome," Hooker intended as a way to parry the blows of Roman apologists. Then as now, Protestants raised with flimsy caricatures of Rome's teachings could easily have their faith shaken by an encounter with the genuine article. Hooker knew that the best way to confirm his hearers in authentic Protestant doctrine was to offer as precise and truthful an account of actual Roman teaching as possible. Did this involve minimizing differences? Hooker did not think so, insisting in his defense against Travers that "it will not be found when it cometh to the balance a light difference where we disagree, as I did acknowledge that we do 'about the very essence of the medicine, whereby Christ cureth our disease.'"[13]

For all of these reasons, although Roman teaching has evolved and dogmatists like Travers are a rarer breed than once they were, Hooker's *Learned Discourse* retains immense value for the contemporary church. In it, we find crisply and frankly stated the true nature of the central conflict between Rome and Protestantism on the doctrine of salvation, at least as it stood between Trent and Vatican II. In it, moreover, we find an extremely useful toolkit for navigating theological differences of any kind in Hooker's lucid distinction between "direct denial" and "denial by logical consequence." In Travers's harsh overreaction to Hooker, we have a reminder of just how easy it is for personal hostility and a habit of suspicion to lead us to read and hear others uncharitably, generating fierce theological conflicts where there turns out to be little substantive disagreement. And in Hooker's grace-filled response, articulating as it does an earnest desire that "God may be merciful to save men even when they err," we find a model for a theology that combines scholastic rigor and precision with warm piety and Christian charity, a theology that takes disagreement and error seriously, while holding out hope in a God whose grace can triumph over all our failures.

---

[13] Richard Hooker, *Master Hookers Answer to the Supplication that Master Travers made to the Counsell*, in *Tractates and Sermons*, ed. Yeandle, 238 (spelling modernized).

EDITORIAL APPROACH

THIS volume is not the first product of The Davenant Institute's quest to present Richard Hooker's work in modern English. Previously, we have published Books I–IV of Hooker's *Laws of Ecclesiastical Polity*—first in four slim, separate volumes, then in a collected and tidied format, published in 2019. This collection of part of the *Laws* is Volume I of an eventual three-volume edition of the entire work.

Our approach to modernizing Hooker's prose in this volume has remained the same as in the *Laws*. Modernizing Hooker's prose is a complex task, certainly more complicated than updating a few archaic words and breaking apart a few lengthy sentences. Hooker's sentences are not just lengthy; his syntax is dense and unwieldy, even by sixteenth-century standards, and so the majority of sentences required syntactical reworking of some kind. Hooker's idioms and turns of phrase are also frequently archaic or rhetorically elevated in Shakespearean ways that can be obscure to the modern reader, so our vocabulary updates were extensive. Our project is therefore a deep and pervasive one, with the outcome being more akin to a *translation* than a modernization.

In general, our method was as follows. Rhys Laverty and Ken Cook would carefully rewrite Hooker's prose from

EDITORIAL APPROACH

scratch, translating Hooker's meaning and prose into modern parlance as best as they were able, and highlighting particularly difficult sections. Second, at a later date, Brad Littlejohn, as the scholarly expert in Hooker's work, would sit down to review the initial translation, adjusting as necessary and ensuring that the logic of Hooker's argument continued to shine through the modernized prose. After this, three of us—Rhys Laverty, Brad Littlejohn, and Onsi Kamel—would review all the work so far, ensuring the elegant flow of both logic and prose, as well as discussing how to translate some of the work's most obscure and difficult phrases and passages. Jonathan Cleland also made a sterling contribution in adding footnotes, and chasing up sources quoted or alluded to by Hooker, many of which were a challenge to pin down.

Since our goal in this "translation" process was to render Hooker's prose easily accessible to a modern audience, we adopted a method that in traditional terms would be considered dynamic rather than literal. The goal was to convey Hooker's *meaning* as accurately and intuitively as possible to a modern audience. We felt free to use reasonably modern colloquialisms, though we also eschewed any words or phrases that smacked entirely of the current century. Such phrases draw attention to themselves, rather than to the underlying text. In certain cases, we pored long over some obsolete word of Hooker's, puzzling and ruminating until we came upon a replacement which served its purpose but did not detract from the elegance of the original.

Devotees of Hooker's original will, we hope, find that we have kept Hooker's rhetoric and tone of voice alive and well in these pages. One of the greatest challenges was honoring Hooker's characteristically long sentences, which are often a delicately balanced collection of mutually dependent clauses, carrying the freight of numerous lines of thought from his preceding argument. Where possible, we did our utmost to preserve such sentences where the basic phrasing and rhetorical cadence were still comprehensible—and indeed, large sections have been left virtually untouched. Yet if, in a modernization, one attempts to keep all such sentences unbroken, it comes to feel rather like trying to keep wet tissue paper in one piece. Therefore, many of Hooker's long sentences have been broken up, but in a way which we are confident retains the sophistication and vigor of his original delivery.

For capitalization, we took the same approach as in the *Laws* regarding the word "Church." Our general rule was to capitalize the word when the universal Church (invisible or visible) was in view, and not to capitalize when a particular church (local or national) was in view; however, "Church of Rome," when referring to the organized institution, was capitalized. Likewise, adjectival constructions, like "church government," were not capitalized.

Regarding italicization, we have italicized text in instances where Hooker provides a list (i.e., "*firstly...secondly*," etc.), and at certain key points of emphasis. Given that (i) this work was originally delivered as a trio of sermons, and (ii) Hooker often deploys a very precise form of reasoning where emphasis of a particular nuance is key, such a use of italics felt appropriate to the nature of the work.

Given that the *Learned Discourse* began life as three sermons, and was then published as a single pamphlet, the original text does not contain chapter divisions. Therefore, the chapter divisions and titles found in this volume are original to us. We felt their insertion was a necessary aid to the reader, illuminating the steps and structure of Hooker's argument by outlining the specific objection that he addresses at each stage. It can also be difficult for the unwary reader to always discern where Hooker is summarizing an objection, or a line of argument that he is about to debunk, and where he is speaking as it were in his own voice. Accordingly, we have been somewhat free about inserting phrases such as "Some might object," etc., in order to better clarify the progression of the argument.

Examples of Changes

Below are a few examples to give a sense of cases when extensive reworking was sometimes necessary, of when an archaism had to be replaced with something contemporary yet not overly modern, and of when almost no change at all was called for.

In some instances, the length of sentences, complexity of syntax, archaism of language, and indeed archaism of thought all conspire to render comprehension quite difficult for the contemporary reader. For example:

> Whereupon I conclude that, although in the first kind no man liveth that sinneth not, and in, the second, as perfect as any do live may sin, yet since the man who is born of God hath a promise that in him the seed of God shall abide, which seed is a sure preservative against the sins of the third suit, greater and clearer assurance we cannot have of anything than of this, that from such sins God shall preserve the righteous, as the apple of his eye, for ever. Directly we deny the foundation of faith, is plain infidelity. Where faith is entered,

> there infidelity is for ever excluded. Therefore by him who hath once sincerely believed in Christ the foundation of Christian faith can never be directly denied. (*Original*, 1.26)

> Therefore, I conclude that although in the first way listed above, there is no man alive who does not sin, and in the second way, even the most perfect man alive may sin—yet since the man who is born of God has a promise that the seed of God shall "abideth in him" (1 Jn. 3:9)—this seed is a sure preservative against the sins of the third kind. We cannot have any greater and clearer assurance than this: that God shall preserve the righteous, the apple of his eye, from such sins forever. To directly deny the foundation of faith is plain infidelity; but wherever faith has entered a life, infidelity is excluded forever. Therefore, the foundation of Christian faith can never be directly denied by anyone who has once sincerely believed in Christ. (*Our version*, p. 44)

A great many changes consisted of breaking down Hooker's lengthy single sentences into shorter ones, whilst retaining (and, we might say tentatively, at times improving) a sense of flow by replacing his somewhat repetitive "ands" with other connective phrases. For instance:

> When we had last the Epistle of St. Paul to the Hebrews in our hands, and of that epistle these words, "In these last days he hath spoken unto us by his Son"; [Heb 1:2] after we had thence collected the nature of the visible Church of Christ, and had defined

it to be a community of men sanctified through the profession of that truth which God hath taught the world by his Son; and had declared that the scope of Christian doctrine is the comfort of them whose hearts are overcharged with the burden of sin; and had proved that the doctrine professed in the Church of Rome doth bereave men of comfort, both in their lives and at their deaths; the conclusion in the end whereunto we came was this… (*Original*, I.9)

Remember when we last considered St. Paul's Epistle to the Hebrews, and especially these words, that God "hath at the end of these days spoken unto us in his Son" (Heb. 1:2). In that sermon, I discussed the nature of the visible Church of Christ and defined it as a community of men who are sanctified through the profession of that truth which God has taught the world by his Son. I also declared that the purpose of Christian doctrine is to comfort those whose hearts are overwhelmed by the burden of sin, and proved that the doctrine professed in the Church of Rome deprives men of comfort both during their lives and at their deaths. The conclusion to which we came at the end was this… (*Our version*, p. 13)

Elsewhere, our changes related chiefly to archaic or obscure phrases. For instance:

As grace may be increased by the merit of good works, so it may be diminished by the demerit of sins venial; it may be lost by

> mortal sin. Inasmuch, therefore, as it is needful in the one case to repair, in the other to recover, the loss which is made, the infusion of grace hath her sundry after-meals; for which cause they make many ways to apply the infusion of grace. (*Original*, I.5)

> As grace may be increased by the merit of good works, so it may be diminished by the demerit of venial sins, and lost entirely by mortal sin. Since it is necessary in the first case to repair, and in the second to recover, the loss which has been experienced, infused grace needs many fresh injections, and they describe many ways by which grace may be re-applied. (*Our version*, p. 6)

We debated the merits of translating "sundry after-meals" as "booster shots," but this felt too colloquial. "Injections" served the purpose well, with both "sundry" and "after-meals" being archaic, obsolete phrases.

Of course, in many instances, Hooker's towering rhetorical ability meant that there was virtually no need for us to edit him, barring small modernizing tweaks. For instance:

> Let it be counted folly, or phrensy, or fury, or whatsoever. It is our wisdom and our comfort; we care for no knowledge in the world but this: that man hath sinned and God hath suffered; that God hath made himself the sin of men, and that men are made the righteousness of God. (*Original*, I.6)

> Let this be counted folly or frenzy, or fury, or whatever you please. It is our wisdom and our comfort; we desire no other

> knowledge in the world but this: that man
> has sinned and God has suffered; that God
> has made himself the sin of men, and that
> men are made the righteousness of God.
> (*Our version*, pp. 8–9)

Textual Notes

The foundation text for Hooker's *Learned Discourse* is widely available, and a free copy is available at the "Online Library of Liberty."[1] This represents a digitization of the seventh edition of Keble's 1832 edition of Hooker's *Works*, revised by the Very Rev. R. W. Church and the Rev. F. Paget in three volumes (Oxford: Clarenden Press, 1888).

The section numbers throughout reflect the "paragraph" numbers provided by John Keble in his 1832 edition, which have been adopted as standard in all subsequent editions of Hooker's work. You will note that we also sometimes included additional paragraph breaks within these numbered sections, here too following the precedent established by the edition on the Online Library of Liberty, as we found that more frequent paragraph breaks improved readability.

In a few places where Hooker quoted loosely from Scripture or an ancient source, or used his own idiosyncratic translation, we chose to follow (and as necessary modernize) his version rather than quoting from a standard modern translation and reference it accordingly. Likewise, all scripture quotations are from the American Standard Version, and all Apocryphal quotations from the Revised Standard Version, unless otherwise noted.

---

[1] URL as of March 9, 2022: https://oll.libertyfund.org/title/keble-the-works-of-richard-hooker-vol-3

LEARNED DISCOURSE OF JUSTIFICATION

We have tried to be very sparse in making any editorial interjections beyond what is strictly necessary, but you will find one or two places where we found an explanatory note in order, without which Hooker's meaning was likely to remain opaque to most readers.

I:
THE REAL DISAGREEMENT BETWEEN ROME AND PROTESTANTISM

"The wicked doth compass about the righteous; therefore justice goeth forth perverted." (Habakkuk 1:4)

1. TO BETTER understand the Prophet's meaning in this passage, we must *first* consider "the wicked," of whom he says that they "compass about the righteous." *Secondly*, we must consider "the righteous" that are compassed about by them. And *finally*, we must consider that which results: "therefore justice goeth forth perverted." Concerning the first question, there are two kinds of wicked men. The blessed Apostle speaks concerning them in 1 Corinthians 5 in this fashion: "For what have I to do with judging them that are without? Do not ye judge them that are within?" (1 Cor. 5:12). There are wicked men, therefore, whom the Church may judge, and there are wicked men whom only God may judge. There are wicked men both inside and outside the walls of the Church. If we find within the Church particular people who appear to be wicked but cannot be brought to repentance, the rule of apostolic judgment is this:

"Separate yourselves from them." If we find whole communities of such people, the rule is this: "Separate yourselves from among them, for what communion hath light with darkness?" (2 Cor. 6:14–17). But the wicked to whom the Prophet refers (in Hab. 1:4) were pagan Babylonians, who therefore were outside of the people of God. We have heard at length before how, for this reason, the Prophet urged God to judge them.

2. Now concerning the righteous, there is not now, nor ever was, any human being absolutely righteous in himself, free from any unrighteousness or sin. We dare not make even the Blessed Virgin herself an exception to this—we would prefer to follow St. Augustine's advice and remain silent on this point for the sake of the honor we owe her as the mother of our Lord and Savior Christ.[1] But since the Roman schools have made this an issue, we must answer with Eusebius Emissenus, who speaks of her and to her to this effect:

> By exclusive privilege your body provided
> hospitality for the hope of all the ends of

---

[1] Hooker is here making reference to Augustine's comment in *On Nature and Grace*. Here, Augustine records those that Pelagius claims lived without sin. Although Augustine denies this claim for the rest of the list, he avoids speaking about the state of Mary. Augustine writes, "Therefore, I make an exception of the Blessed Virgin Mary, in whose case, out of respect for the Lord, I wish to raise no question at all when the discussion concerns sins—for whence do we know what an abundance of grace for entirely overcoming sin was conferred on her who had the merit to conceive and bear him who undoubtedly was without sin?" Augustine, "On Nature and Grace," in *Four Anti-Pelagian Writings*, trans. John A. Mourant and William J. Collinge, Fathers of the Church 86 (Washington, D.C.: The Catholic University of America Press, 1992), 36.42, pp. 52–54 (PL 44:0267).

I

the earth, the honor of the world and the common joy of all men for nine months. He from whom all things had their beginning had his own beginning by means of you. From your body he received the blood which was to be shed for the life of the world. From you he took that which— even for you—he paid. *A peccati enim veteris nexu, per se non est immunis nec ipsa genitrix Redemptoris*: "The mother of the Redeemer herself, otherwise than by redemption, is not loosed from the bonds of original sin" *(Second Homily on the Nativity of the Lord)*.[2]

If Christ has paid a ransom for all (1 Tim. 2:6), including even her, it follows that all without exception were captives. If one has died for all, then all were dead, dead in sin (2 Cor. 5:14, Eph. 2:1–10). If all were sinful, then none were absolutely righteous in themselves; but we are absolutely righteous in Christ (2 Cor. 5:21). If the world would know what a perfectly righteous man looks like, then it must behold a Christian man, for Christ "was made unto us wisdom from

---

[2] This section comes from the Eusebius Gallicanus, a collection of seventy-six sermons by early church writers. The authorship of the sermons is unknown, although they have been attributed to a variety of authors. Here, Hooker is referring to the second sermon, entitled *Homilia II de natale Domini* (also known as *De nativitate Domini*, i.e., The Nativity of the Lord). For the section cited here, see *Homilia II*, in *Eusebius 'Gallicanus': Collectio homiliarum*, ed. Fr. Glorie, Corpus Christianorum: Series Latina 101 (Turnholti: Brepols, 1970), 4, p. 26. Hooker mentions that the author is Eusebius, and although this may be a possibility, there is no way to know for certain who the author of this text is. The Eusebius Hooker refers to was the Bishop of Emesa and was well-known for learning and eloquence. He was the student of his namesake, Eusebius of Caesarea (260/265–339/340), the great church historian and biographer of Constantine the Great (c. 272–337).

God, and righteous and sanctification, and redemption" (1 Cor. 1:30). He is our wisdom because he has revealed his Father's will; he is our justice because he has offered himself as a sacrifice for sin; he is our sanctification because he has given us his Spirit; he is our redemption because he has appointed a day to vindicate his children out of the bondage of corruption into glorious liberty. How Christ is made our wisdom and redemption may be discussed when occasion arises. But how Christ is made the righteousness of mankind, we will discuss in what follows.

3. There is a glorifying righteousness for men in the world to come; and there is a justifying and a sanctifying righteousness here and now. The righteousness with which we shall be clothed in the world to come is both perfect and inherent. That righteousness by which we are now justified is perfect, but not inherent. That righteousness by which we are sanctified is inherent, but not perfect. These distinctions will make it easier to understand that great question which stands between the Church of England and the Church of Rome regarding the righteousness that justifies before God.

4. First, although the Roman Church imagines that the mother of our Lord and Savior Jesus Christ was, for his honor, and by his special protection, completely preserved from all sin, they nonetheless teach—as we do—that all have sinned. They teach that infants who have never actually sinned have defiled natures, destitute of justice, and turned away from God. They teach, as we do, that God alone justifies the soul of man without any other cooperative cause of justice—that is, in making man righteous, none work effectively alongside God in this matter, but rather, that God works alone. They teach, as we do, that no one has ever attained justification but by the merits of Jesus Christ. They

I

teach, as we do, that although Christ as God is the efficient cause of our justification and that Christ as man is the meritorious cause of our justification, something nonetheless is required of us as well. God is the cause of our natural life; we live in him (Acts 17:28). However, he does not give life to our bodies without giving life to the soul within the body as well. Christ's merits have made us just before God. But, just as medicine does not heal by being made available but by being applied, so there can be no justification for mankind apart from the application of the merit of Christ. Thus far we join hands with the Church of Rome.

5. Where, then, do we disagree? We disagree about the very nature of the medicine by which Christ cures our disease; we disagree about the way in which he applies it; and we disagree about the number and the power of the means which God requires in us in order to effectually apply this medicine to comfort our souls.

When we ask them what the righteousness is that justifies a Christian man, they answer that it is a divine spiritual quality. Further, they teach that when this quality is received within the soul, it first makes one to be born of God (cf. Jn. 1:13), and then endows the soul with power to bring forth those works which are proper to those who are born of God (this happens, they say, in just the same way that the soul of a man, being joined to his body, first makes him a rational creature, and then enables him to perform the functions which are proper to rational creatures). They teach that this quality renders the soul gracious and pleasing in the sight of God (thus its name, "grace"), and that by this grace, through the merit of Christ we are delivered from sin and likewise from its consequences: eternal death and condemnation.

They understand this grace to be applied to the soul by infusion. They make this comparison: just as the body is warmed by the heat which is within it, so the soul becomes righteous by an inherent grace, a grace that can increase—as the body might become more and more warm, so the soul may become more and more justified, as grace increases. Furthermore, they argue that this increase of grace is merited by good works, just as good works are made meritorious by it. Thus, in their doctrine, the first reception of grace into the soul is the "first justification," and the increase of this grace is the "second justification."

As grace may be increased by the merit of good works, so it may be diminished by the demerit of venial sins, and lost entirely by mortal sin. Since it is necessary in the first case to repair, and in the second to recover, the loss which has been experienced, infused grace needs many fresh injections, and they describe many ways by which grace may be re-applied. For instance, it is applied to infants without either faith or works through baptism, so as to take away original sin as well as the punishment due such sin. For adult unbelievers and wicked men, it is applied in their first justification through baptism apart from works but not without faith, and takes away both actual sins and original sin, together with all punishments, temporal or eternal, which they had deserved. To those who have obtained this first justification, or first reception of grace, it is further applied by good works. This results in the increase of the first grace, and is the second justification. If they work more and more, grace increases more and more, and they are more and more justified.

To those who have lost some portion of grace by venial sins, it can be re-applied by holy water, *Ave Marias*, the sign of the cross, papal salutations, and the like; these means serve to restore grace that has decayed. To any who have lost grace altogether through mortal sin, it can be re-applied by the so-called sacrament of penance, which has the power to confer grace anew, although not to fully restore the grace that has been lost. For penance can only cleanse the stain or guilt of sin actually committed, and change an eternal punishment into a temporal punishment to be borne in this life, if there is enough time at least. If not, the punishment must be endured in the hereafter, though it can be lightened by masses, works of charity, pilgrimages, fasts, and the like, or else pardoned in part or in full by church authorities.

This is, in short, the mystery of the "Man of Sin" (2 Thes. 2:3–4), the maze which the Church of Rome sets her followers to tread when they ask her the way of justification. I cannot take time now to take this building down and sift it piece by piece. Instead, I will simply aim to lay out the structure of apostolic teaching in a few words, so that, as befell Dagon in the presence of the Ark (1 Sam. 5), so it may befall the Roman "Babylon" in the presence of what God has established.

6. "Yea verily," says the Apostle, "I count all things to be loss for the excellency of the knowledge of Chist Jesus my Lord: for whom I suffered the loss of all things, and do count them but refuse, that I may gain Christ, and be found in him, not having a righteousness of mine own, even that which is of the law, but that which is through faith in Christ, the righteousness which is from God by faith" (Phil. 3:8–9). Whether they speak of the first or second justification, they make the essence of it an inherent divine quality, that is, a righteousness which is in us. But if it is in us, then it is ours as our souls are ours, even if we have our souls from God

and can possess them no longer than pleases him. For if God withdraws the breath from our nostrils, we return to dust at once. But the righteousness in which we must be found, if we are to be justified, is not our own. Therefore, we cannot be justified by any inherent quality. Rather, *Christ has merited righteousness for as many as are found in him.* God finds us in him, if we are faithful, for by faith we are incorporated into Christ.

Thus, although we ourselves are altogether sinful and unrighteous, even the man who is himself impious, full of iniquity and sin, if he is found in Christ through faith and hates his sin in repentance, God beholds him with a gracious eye! God puts away his sin by not imputing it to him; God takes away the punishment he justly deserves by pardoning it; God accepts him in Jesus Christ as perfectly righteous, as if he had fulfilled all that is commanded in the law, and—can it be?—as *more* perfectly righteous than if he himself had fulfilled the whole law!

I must take care in my words, but the Apostle Paul himself says, "Him who knew no sin he made to be sin on our behalf; that we might become the righteousness of God in him" (2 Cor. 5:21). Thus, we are, in the sight of God the Father, as the very Son of God himself! Let this be counted folly or frenzy, or fury, or whatever you please. It is our wisdom and our comfort; we desire no other knowledge in the world but this: that man has sinned and God has suffered; that God has made himself the sin of men, and that men are made the righteousness of God.

You see therefore that the Church of Rome, in teaching justification by inherent grace, perverts the truth of Christ, and that from the hands of the very Apostles we have received a different teaching than Rome's.

I

Now when it comes to the righteousness of sanctification, we do not deny that it is inherent, and we acknowledge that unless we work at a holy life, we do not have it. However, we distinguish the righteousness of sanctification as something different in nature from the righteousness of justification. We are righteous in one way by the faith of Abraham (Gen. 15:1–6); in regard to the other way, unless we do the works of Abraham, we are not righteous (Gen. 22:1–14). Of justification, St. Paul says, "But to him that worketh not, but believeth on him that justifieth the ungodly, his faith is reckoned for righteousness" (Rom. 4:5). Of sanctification, St. John says, *Qui facit justitiam, justus est*—"He that doeth righteousness is righteous" (1 Jn. 3:7). Of justification, St. Paul proves by the example of Abraham that we have it by faith without works (Rom. 4:1–25). Of sanctification, St. James teaches by the example of Abraham "that we have it by works, and not only by faith" (James 2:14–26). St. Paul clearly distinguishes these two parts of Christian righteousness from one another. In Romans 6 he writes, "But now being made free from sin and become servants to God, ye have your fruit unto sanctification, and the end eternal life" (Rom. 6:22). "Made free from sin and become servants to God"—this is the righteousness of justification. "Fruit unto santification"—this is the righteousness of sanctification. By the first we gain the right of inheritance; by the second we are brought into the actual possession of eternal bliss. And so the end of both of these is everlasting life.

7. Let us come back to the Prophet Habakkuk. He refers to the Jews as "righteous men," not only because, being justified by faith, they were free from sin, but also because they bore fruit in holy living. He provides us with an example of charitable judgment, leaving it to God to discern what

men are, and speaking of them according to what they profess themselves to be—even though men are not holy based on what other men think of them but based on what God knows to be the case. But every Christian man must understand that, in a spirit of Christian equity, he is bound to think and speak of his brothers as men who have a measure of holiness and a right to the titles with which God—by his special favor and mercy—condescends to honor his chosen servants. That is why we see the Apostles of our Savior Christ refer to the people of God by the title of "saints"; likewise, the Prophet refers to the faithful of his day as "righteous." But let us all endeavor to be in fact what we desire to be called. "Godly names do not justify godless men," says Salvianus.[3] We deserve rebuke when we are honored with names and titles which do not match our lives and manners.

If, indeed, we have lives characterized by the fruit of holiness, we must note that the more we abound in holy living, the more we need to desire to be strengthened and supported in our endeavor. Even our virtues may become snares to us. The enemy that waits on all occasions to work our ruin (1 Pet. 5:8) has always found it harder to overthrow a humble sinner than a proud saint. No one's situation is as perilous as that of the man whom Satan has persuaded to trust his own righteousness to present him pure and blameless in the sight of God (compare Jude 24–25). Even if we could say that "we feel no guilt in our own consciences"

---

[3] Salvianus, also known as Salvian, was a fifth-century theologian who served for a period as presbyter in Marseilles. The work being cited is *De gubernatione Dei* (On the Government of God) 19.90 (PL 53:0092A). The Latin phrase, *reatus impii est pium nomen*, is cited by Hooker before he offers his English translation/paraphrase.

I

(which no one could honestly say, for we know ourselves to be far from such innocence), could we plead "Not guilty!" in the presence of our Judge, who sees further into our hearts than we ourselves are able to see? Even if our hands had never done violence to our brothers, a violent thought proves us murderers before him. If we had never opened our mouths to utter any scandalous, offensive, or hurtful word, the cry of our secret thoughts still echoes in God's ears. If we did not commit the evils which we do daily and hourly—the evil deeds, words, or thoughts—consider how many defects are intermingled with even the good things we do!

When it comes to our actions, God has special regard for the mind and intentions of the one who acts. If we then eliminate all those deeds in which we aimed at our own glory, sought to please men, or satisfy our own pleasures, we will find the number of those things which we do without ulterior motives, purely for the love of God, is very small indeed. Let us consider the holiest and best thing we do: prayer. We are never more focused on God than when we pray, yet how often when we pray, we find our thoughts and desires distracted! How little reverence we show to the grand majesty of that God to whom we speak! How little remorse for our own failures! How little we taste the sweet influence of his tender mercies! Are we not, often, so unwilling to begin prayer and so glad to end it that it is as if God had laid a great burden upon us in saying, "Call upon me"!

What I say may seem somewhat extreme, so let everyone consider only what his own heart tells him. I only ask this: suppose God would grant us—not as in the case of Abraham at Sodom, fifty, forty, thirty, twenty, or even just ten good persons so that the city should not be destroyed (Gen. 18:22–33)—but a different offer. Suppose it was one like this: "Search all the generations of men since the Fall of our father Adam, and find one man who has done any single pure action without any stain or blemish, and for that one man's singular act, neither man nor angel shall feel the torments which are prepared for both." Do you think that this ransom—fit to deliver men and angels—could actually be found among the sons of men? Even the *best* things we do have something in them that requires pardon! How then can anything we do be meritorious and worthy of reward?

It is true that God graciously promises to give all the gifts of a blessed life to as many as sincerely keep his Law (e.g., Dt. 11:13–15), although they are not able to keep it strictly (Josh. 24:19–21). Therefore we acknowledge the necessary duty of doing good works, but we utterly renounce any notion of meritoriousness for these good actions. We see how far we are from the perfect righteousness of the Law. The little fruit we have in holiness is, God knows, corrupt and unsound. We can put no confidence in it at all, nor make any demands based on it, and we dare not call God to a reckoning as if we had him in our debt. Our continual plea to him is, and must be, "Please bear with our infirmities. Pardon our offenses."

8. But the people of whom the Prophet Habakkuk speaks—were they all, or even a majority of them, careful to walk uprightly? Did they thirst after righteousness (Mt. 5:6)? Did they wish, did they long with the righteous Prophet, "Oh that my ways were established to observe thy statutes" (Ps. 119:5)? Did they lament with the righteous Apostle, "Wretched men that we are! The good which we wish and purpose and strive to do, we cannot do" (Rom.

7:18–19, 24)? No. The words of other Prophets about this people show the opposite. How grievously Isaiah mourns over them: "Ah sinful nation, a people laden with iniquity, a seed of evil-doers, children that deal corruptly!" (Is. 1:4). Nonetheless, God's profound compassion for us is such that he does not deny us, not even when we are laden with iniquity, permission to call upon him as a Father, to seek his aid and entreat his help that whatever plagues we have deserved, we may still be spared, and that we might not be hemmed in by pagans and unbelievers.

The Jerusalem of Habakkuk's day was a sinful, polluted city, but it was still righteous compared to Babylon. And shall the righteous be overwhelmed, shall they be utterly compassed about by the wicked? The Prophet not only complains, "Lord, how has it come to pass that you treat us so severely (we who are called by your name) and overlook the heathen nations which despise you?" No, he is driven into extreme grief and goes so far as to conclude that what has occurred is wicked; it is wickedness for the righteous to be treated in this fashion: "Justice goeth forth perverted" (Hab. 1:4).

9. This conclusion has many lessons which would be valuable for you to hear, and for me to speak, if necessity did not require me to focus on another task. When Paul and Barnabas were asked to preach the same things a second time, they considered it their duty to satisfy these godly desires of men sincerely inclined toward the truth (Acts 13:13–43). Likewise, hopefully it will not seem burdensome to me or unprofitable for you if I follow their example, since a similar occasion has been offered to me. Remember when we last considered St. Paul's Epistle to the Hebrews, and especially these words, that God "hath at the end of these

days spoken unto us in his Son" (Heb. 1:2). In that sermon, I discussed the nature of the visible Church of Christ and defined it as a community of men who are sanctified through the profession of that truth which God has taught the world by his Son. I also declared that the purpose of Christian doctrine is to comfort those whose hearts are overwhelmed by the burden of sin, and proved that the doctrine professed in the Church of Rome deprives men of comfort both during their lives and at their deaths. The conclusion to which we came at the end was this:

> Since the Church of Rome is so corrupted in matters of faith and refuses to reform herself, we are to utterly separate ourselves from her. The example of our forefathers cannot suffice to keep us in communion and fellowship with that church in the hope that we might be saved in this communion, just because our forefathers were. I have no doubt that God was merciful to save thousands of them, even though they lived in popish superstitions, because they sinned ignorantly. As for us, however, the truth is now laid before our eyes.

I plead with you to take notice of my words, "I have no doubt that *God was merciful to save thousands of our fathers who lived in popish superstitions, because they sinned ignorantly*." Examine these words with your most exacting judgment. If they be found as gold, let them stand, suitable for the precious foundation on which they were laid (cf. 1 Cor. 3:10–4:5). But if they are found to be hay or stubble, my own hand shall set fire to it!

I

Two questions have arisen with regard to this former sermon of mine. The first is: "Whether our fathers—infected as they were with popish errors and superstitions—might be saved at all?" The second is: "Whether their ignorance might serve as a reason for us to think that they might be saved?" We will therefore examine first, what *possibility*, and then second, what *probability* there is that God might be merciful to so many of our forefathers.

II:
COULD OUR FATHERS BE SAVED?

10. SOME object: could so many of our fathers living in popish superstitions be saved by the mercy of God? Surely this could not be! After all, God has spoken to his people by means of an angel from heaven concerning Babylon (and "Babylon" we understand as a reference to the Church of Rome): "Come forth, my people, out of her, that ye have no fellowship with her sins and that ye receive not of her plagues" (Rev. 18:4; cf. 16:17–18:24). In responding to this objection, I would first concede, that I do not understand these words to refer only to temporal suffering, like physical death, sorrow, famine, and the fire to which God had wrathfully condemned Babylon. Rather, I agree that in order to save his chosen people he says, "Come forth!" in the same fashion as in the Gospel, speaking of Jerusalem's desolations, he says, "Let them that are in Judea flee to the mountains, and let them that are in the midst of her depart out" (Luke 21:21); or as the angel warned Lot in former times, "Arise, take thy wife, and thy two daughters that are here, lest thou be consumed in the iniquity of the city!" (Gen. 19:15). Since the passage in Revelation says, "Come forth, my people, out of her, that ye have no fellowship with her sins and that ye receive not of her plagues," I take these

plagues to mean the eternal plagues which the sins of Babylon deserve, which necessarily implies the everlasting destruction of all those who participate in Babylon's sins. How then could it be possible for so many of our fathers to be saved, since they were so far from departing out of "Babylon," but rather took the Church of Rome for their mother, and died in her bosom?

11. The first thing to note in response to this objection is that, although the plagues are threatened on all those who participate in the sins of Babylon, we can say nothing about how this applies to our forefathers unless we first show what the sins of Babylon are, and what it means to participate in them so as to incur these everlasting plagues. We must draw a sharp distinction between these sins and sins which are common to both those inside and outside of the Church of Rome. When the Scripture says, "Come forth, my people, out of her, that ye have no fellowship with her sins," this plainly refers to sins of such a nature that we can only avoid by decisively separating ourselves from Babylon. These are impieties which they have established by law and to which all among them must either assent, or at least, by threat of force, give an outward appearance of assent. For example, the Church of Rome claims that the same credit and reverence which we give to the Scriptures of God should also be given to their unwritten traditions. Similarly, they understand the Pope as the supreme spiritual head over the universal Church militant, and that the bread in the Eucharist is transubstantiated into Christ, such that it is to be adored, and offered to God as a propitiatory sacrifice for the living and the dead! Likewise, they hold that images are to be worshipped, that the saints are to be called upon as intercessors between God and man, and so on.

Now some heresies concern only things believed, like the transubstantiation of the sacramental elements in the Eucharist, while others concern things which are also practiced and put in use, like the adoration of transubstantiated bread and wine. So we must note that even when such practices are sometimes erroneously received, the underlying doctrine is not always heretically embraced. Now I say that everyone who knows of a heresy and allows it—by word or deed—is a partaker in the maintenance of that heresy, whether or not he knows it to be a heresy. All the more so are they participants who, most dangerously of all, know heresy to be heresy and still deceptively and outwardly permit that which they inwardly condemn. But heresy is heretically maintained only by those who obstinately hold it even after receiving wholesome admonitions. Concerning this last group, as well as the second, I have no doubt that, without actual repentance, their condemnation *is* inevitable. So if anyone thought that in speaking of our forefathers, I referred to all of them without discrimination, please take note of my words carefully: "I have no doubt that God was merciful to save *thousands* of our fathers." Now, with God's help, I will try to make this clearer.

12. There are many people who are participants in error without holding the heresy of the Church of Rome. The ordinary people who followed their leaders, observing what they did and doing what was required of them, thought that they were giving good service to God, when in fact they were dishonoring him. This was their error. But with regard to the *heresies* of the Church of Rome, that is to say, their formal doctrines contrary to Christian truth, what one person out of ten thousand ever even understood them? Even those who understood and accepted Roman heresies were

II

not all equally guilty of participating in them. Some of those who accepted them were indeed their original founders and establishers; but only their Popes and Councils were guilty of this. The ordinary people had nothing to do with this! Further, among those who maintain popish heresy by receiving it from others, only a few have been teachers of it. These are not the ordinary people, only their preachers and schoolmen. Even among those guilty of *teaching* popish heresies, we may draw a distinction, for not all have been teachers of *all* popish heresies! "Recognize a difference with some," St. Jude says, "and have compassion on them" (Jude 22).[1]

Shall we consider them all equally compromised? Shall we cast them all headlong? Shall we throw them all into that infernal and ever-flaming lake (Rev. 20:14)? Shall we treat those that have been participants in the error of Babylon the same way as those who are heretical insiders? Shall we treat those who have been the authors of heresy the same as those who were compelled by terror and violence to receive it? What about those who taught it, compared to those simple ones who have been seduced to believe it by the cunning and cleverness of false teachers? Is there no difference between those participants in one heresy, and those who have been partakers in many, or between those who have partaken in many, and those who have embraced them all?

13. Nonetheless, although the condemnation due to some is lighter than that due to others, still I grant that from the man who plowed his fields, to the one who sat in the

---

[1] Here, we have not quoted from the ASV, due to its notable difference from Hooker's original quotation, and out of a desire to preserve his syntax. The language that Hooker uses here paraphrases the 1560 Geneva Bible.

Vatican, all these partakers in the sins of Babylon deserved temporal punishments, even those who were merely practicing errors that their heretical leaders taught. When the blind lead the blind, both ordinarily end up in a pit (Mt. 15:14)!

But woe be the hour of our birth, unless we might persuade ourselves of better things, things that accompany men's salvation (Hebrews 6:9), even where we know that worse things—things that accompany condemnation—are deserved! So we must show some way how our fathers might possibly have escaped condemnation.

What way is there for sinners to escape God's judgment other than by appealing to the seat of God's saving mercy? We do not, like Origen, extend such mercy to devils and damned spirits![2] God has mercy upon thousands, but there are thousands, likewise, who are hardened. Christ, therefore, has set the boundaries and fixed the limits of his saving mercy within the following boundaries. In the third chapter of St. John's Gospel, mercy is limited to believers: "For God sent not the Son into the world to judge the world; but that the world should be saved through him. He that believeth on him is not judged: he that believeth not hath been judged already, because he hath not believed on the name of the only begotten Son of God" (Jn. 3:17–18). In Revelation 2, mercy is limited to the penitent, for John says of Jezebel and her followers, "I gave her time that she should repent; and she willeth not to repent of her fornication. Behold, I cast her into a bed, and them that commit adultery with her into great tribulation, except they repent

---

[2] Origen was a third-century Greek theologian who is known for teaching *Apocatastasis*, the belief that all people and spiritual beings will eventually be redeemed and return to God.

II

of her works. And I will kill her children with death" (Rev. 2:21–23). Therefore, any hope for our fathers would be in vain, if they were utterly faithless and unrepentant.

14. However, not all are faithless who are either weak in assenting to the truth, or stubborn in maintaining beliefs in any way opposed to the truth of Christian doctrine. Rather, as many as hold to the precious foundation, as many as have built themselves upon the rock, the foundation of the Church, they shall survive the fiery trial and be saved—even if they only hold it weakly, as by a slender thread; even if they build many contemptible and unsuitable things upon it, things that cannot withstand the trial of fire (1 Cor. 3:10–15). So then, if our fathers did not hold the foundation of faith, there is no doubt that they were faithless. But if many of them did hold it, then there is nothing to prevent these from being saved. Let us see what the foundation of faith is, and whether we may think that thousands of our fathers, although living in popish superstitions, held the foundation nevertheless.

15. If the "foundation of faith" means the general basis upon which we depend when we believe, then the writings of the Evangelists and the Apostles are the foundation of the Christian faith: *Credimus quia legimus*—"We believe that which we read"—says St. Jerome.[3] Oh that the Church of Rome *interpreted* those fundamental writings upon which we

---

[3] Jerome, *De perpetua virginitate Beatae Mariae, adversus Helvidium* 19.227 (PL 23:0203A). For an introduction to and a contemporary English translation of this work, see "On the Perpetual Virginity of the Blessed Mary against Helvidius," in *Dogmatic and Polemical Works*, trans. John N. Hritzu, The Fathers of the Church: A New Translation 53 (Washington, D.C.: The Catholic University of America Press, 1965), 3–46.

build our faith as soundly as she willingly *holds and embraces* them!

16. But if the term "foundation" means the principal thing which we believe, then the foundation of our faith is that which St. Paul proclaims to Timothy: "Christ was manifested in the flesh, justified in the Spirit," etc. (1 Tim. 3:16). Our foundation is Nathaniel's: "Thou art the Son of God; thou art King of Israel" (Jn. 1:49). And the inhabitants of Samaria have the same foundation: "This is Christ, the Savior of the world!" (Jn. 4:42). He that directly denies *this*, utterly destroys the very foundation of our faith.

Thus far, I have proven that, although the Church of Rome has played the harlot worse than Israel ever did, they are not like the synagogue of the Jews which openly denied Jesus Christ and is completely excluded from the New Covenant (Rev. 2:9; 3:9). Consider Samaria and Jerusalem. Samaria compared to Jerusalem is termed *Aholah*, "a church or tabernacle of her own," while Jerusalem is called *Aholibah*, that is, "the resting place of the Lord" (cf. Ezek. 23). So whatever we call the Church of Rome when comparing her to Reformed churches, we still draw a distinction between Rome and heathen communities, as we would between Babylon and Samaria. So let me restate myself. I insist that the Church of Rome, together with all of her children, would be completely excluded from God's favor, and that there would be no difference in the world between our fathers and the Saracens, Turks or pagans, *if* they directly denied Christ crucified for the salvation of the world.

17. But how many millions of them are known to have ended their mortal lives in faith, uttering as they drew their final breath, "Christ, my Savior! My Redeemer, Jesus!" Shall

II

we say that such people did not hold the foundation of the Christian faith?

But some will respond by arguing that although they might have genuinely declared such a faith, they might still be far from salvation. For, behold, the Apostle says, "Behold, I, Paul, say unto you that, if ye are circumcised, Christ will profit you nothing" (Gal. 5:2). Christ alone works man's salvation. The Galatians were cast away by adding circumcision and other rites of the Law to Christ. Just so, the Church of Rome teaches her children to add other things to faith in him. Thus, the objector says, their faith, their belief, profits them nothing.

It is true, indeed, that they join other things with Christ. But how? They do not add anything to the work of redemption itself, for they grant that Christ alone has acted sufficiently for the salvation of the whole world. It is in the application of this inestimable treasure that the additions are made, in its effectual application for their salvation. No matter how modestly they confess that they seek remission of sins in no other way than by the blood of Christ—humbly using the means appointed by him to apply the benefits of his holy blood—they teach, in reality, so many things that are pernicious to the Christian faith that the very foundation of faith which they hold is plainly overthrown, and the meaning and power of the blood of Christ extinguished.

We may therefore dispute with them, press them, and urge them with warnings of consequences as severe as the Apostle Paul's to the Galatians. But I demand to know: if some of those Galatians, heartily embracing the Gospel of Christ and being sincere and sound in faith—apart from this error alone—died before they were ever taught how perilous an opinion they held, should we suppose that the damage of this error outweighed the benefit of their faith, such that the mercy of God might not save them? I grant that the Galatians overthrew the very foundation of faith by logical consequence. But is that not true also even for some things which the Lutheran churches stubbornly maintain at present?

For my own part, therefore, I dare not deny the possibility of the salvation of those who have been the chief instruments of our own salvation, even if they carried to their grave a persuasion so greatly repugnant to the truth. Since, then, it may be said of the Church of Rome that she still has "a little power" (Rev. 3:8), and that she does not directly deny the foundation of Christianity, I may, I trust, without offense to anyone, persuade myself that thousands of our fathers in earlier times, while living and dying within her walls, have found mercy at the hands of God.

18. But what if they did not repent of their errors? God forbid that I should open my mouth and deny what Christ has said: "Except ye repent, ye shall all in like manner perish" (Lk. 13:3). If they did not repent, they perished. But additionally, notice that we have the benefit of a double repentance. The smallest sin which we commit in deed, word, or thought is death apart from repentance. But how many aspects of our deeds, works, and thoughts escape us given our limited knowledge? How many of our sins do we fail to recognize as sins! And without the knowledge and the observation of sin, there is no actual repentance. We cannot but conclude then, that for as many as hold the foundation, and who hate all known sin and error, the blessing of repentance for unknown sins and errors is obtained from the hands of God and through the gracious mediation of Christ

II

Jesus! This is the case for all who cry with the Prophet David, "Clear thou me from hidden faults!" (Ps.19:12).

19. But some will object: this discussion is like washing a wall of dirt; we labor in vain, we've proven nothing that we seek to justify! Even infidels and heathens, after all, are not so godless that they may not cry to God for mercy and have a general desire to have their sins forgiven. But to those who deny the foundation of faith, there can be no salvation—according to the ordinary course of God in saving men—without a specific repentance from that error (Rom. 14:23). The Galatians, thinking that they could not be saved unless they were circumcised, directly overthrew the foundation of faith. Therefore, if any of them died in this persuasion—whether before or after they were told of their error—their case is dreadful. There is but one outcome for them: death and condemnation. For the Apostle says nothing about men who have died, but asserts universally, "If ye receive circumcision, Christ will profit you nothing. Yea, I testify again to every man that receiveth circumcision that he is a debtor to do the whole law. Ye are severed from Christ, ye who would be justified by the law; ye are fallen away from grace" (Gal. 5:2–4).

The same, then, would be the case for those in the Church of Rome. For did not St. Paul speak long ago of those whom Antichrist has seduced? He says, "They received not the love of the truth, that they might be saved. And for this cause God sendeth them a working of error, that they should believe a lie: that they all might be judged who believed not the truth, but had pleasure in unrighteousness" (2 Thes. 2:9–12). And St. John says, "All that dwell on the earth shall worship [the Beast], every one whose name hath not been written from the foundation of the world in the Book of Life" (Rev. 13:8). Indeed, many of them in former times, as their books and writings show, held the foundation—that is, salvation by Christ alone—and therefore might be saved. For God has always had a Church among those who firmly kept his saving truth! But, it will be alleged, those who agree with the Church of Rome that we cannot be saved by Christ alone without works deny the foundation of faith—not by mere logical consequence, but directly. They do not hold the foundation at all,—not by so much as a slender thread.

20. This, if memory serves, sums up all the reasonable objections that have been alleged against my original statement. I hope, then, that once they have been answered, the controversy in question can be ended.

What then of general repentance? Shall a murderer, a blasphemer, an unclean person, a Turk, a Jew, any sinner escape the wrath of God by a general "God forgive me"? Truly, I never supposed that a general repentance serves for all sins or for all sinners. It serves only for the common oversights of our sinful life and for the faults which we either do not notice or do not know to be faults. However, our fathers actually sought to be repentant for sins which they knew displeased God—or else they do not fall within the consideration of my earlier remarks.

Again, that they could not be saved but by embracing the foundation of the Christian faith, we have not only affirmed about them above, but proven. So why can it not be granted that thousands of our fathers, despite living in popish superstitions, could yet, by God's mercy, be saved? There are three ways in which we could reach this conclusion.

II

First, suppose they had directly denied the very foundation of Christianity, and never repented of that sin. Still, when we say that there could be no ordinary means of salvation for them, we thereby say—or at least imply—that they could yet be saved from hell by some extraordinary privilege of God's mercy. But such an argument goes further than necessary for my purposes. *Second*, let us say that the foundation was denied by the force of some heresy which the Church of Rome maintains. Still, consider how many people were there among our fathers who, being seduced by the common error of that church, never knew the meaning of her heresies! So by this means we might say that even if all popish heretics perished, nevertheless thousands of them which lived merely in popish superstitions might be saved. *Third*, since even all that did hold popish heresies did not hold *all* the heresies of the Pope, why might not thousands who were infected with such leaven live and die unsoured by this, and so be saved? *Fourth*, even if they all held this heresy, doubtless many held it only in a general form of words which a favorable interpreter might explain in a sense different from the poisoned ideas of heresy.

For example, did they hold that we cannot be saved by Christ without works? We ourselves, I think, say much the same, understanding salvation as in that verse, *Corde creditur ad justitiam, ore fit confessio ad salutem* ("For with the heart man believeth unto righteousness; and with the mouth confession is made unto salvation," Rom. 10:10). Except for infants and men who die at the moment of their conversion, none shall see God but those who seek peace and holiness—not as a cause of their salvation, but as a way which must be walked by those who will be saved.

Did they hold that without works we are not justified? If we take justification in such a manner that it may also imply sanctification, and St. James says as much (James 2:14–26). For unless there is an ambiguity in some term, St. Paul and St. James contradict each other, which cannot be. Now, there is no ambiguity with the terms "faith" and "works," because both Apostles use these terms in one and the same sense. Therefore, we find that "justification" is spoken of by St. Paul without implying sanctification, when he proves that a man is justified by faith without works (cf. Rom. 3:20–28). Likewise, we find that "justification" sometimes implies sanctification to be joined with it. I suppose, then, that we do best to interpret St. James as speaking not in that prior sense, but in the latter.

21. We have already shown that there are two kinds of Christian righteousness. One is outside of us, which we have by imputation. The other is within us, consisting of faith, hope, charity, and other Christian virtues. St. James proves that Abraham had not only the one, because the thing he believed was imputed to him as righteousness (James 2:23), but also the other, because he offered up his son (James 2:21–22). God gives us both the one righteousness and the other, the one by accepting us as righteous in Christ, and the other by working Christian righteousness in us. The proper and most immediate efficient cause of this latter righteousness in us is the Spirit of adoption which we have received into our hearts (Rom. 8:15).

That which this righteousness consists of, and is really and formally made up of, are those infused virtues which are proper and distinctive to the lives of saints, which the Spirit brings with it, in the very first moment it is given by God. Its effects are those actions as the Apostle calls the

II

fruits, works, or operations of the Spirit (Gal. 5:22–23). The difference between these operations of the Spirit and the root from which they spring makes it necessary to conceive of two kinds of sanctifying righteousness: "habitual" and "actual." "Habitual holiness" is that holiness with which our souls are inwardly endowed from the first moment when we begin to be temples of the Holy Ghost (Eph. 2:18–22). "Actual holiness" is that holiness which continues afterward to beautify all the parts and actions of our life—the holiness for which Enoch, Job, Zechariah, and other saints are so highly commended in the Scriptures.

If, at this point, it is asked which of these we receive first, I answer that we receive all at the same time: the Spirit, the virtues of the Spirit, the habitual justice which is ingrafted, and the external justice of Christ Jesus which is imputed. Whenever we have any one of these, we have them all—they go together. But since no man is justified unless he believes, and no man believes unless he has faith, and no man has faith unless he has received the Spirit of *adoption*, we must hold that imputed righteousness, although in dignity the chiefest gift, is last in the order of belief, faith, and adoption; for though these graces imply justification, justification necessarily presupposes them. Actual righteousness, which is the righteousness of good works, succeeds and follows all the others, both in order and time.

This distinction, being carefully noted, plainly shows how the faith of true believers cannot be divorced from hope and love; how faith is a part of sanctification, and yet necessary for justification; how faith is perfected by good works, and no works of ours are good without faith; and finally, how our fathers might have held that we are justified by faith alone, and yet also have truly held that without good works we are not justified. Did they think that men merit rewards in heaven by the works they perform on earth? The ancient Church Fathers use the term "meriting" for "obtaining," and it is used in the same sense by the Lutherans of Wittenberg in their Confession: "We teach that good works commanded by God are necessarily to be done, and that by the free kindness of God they merit sure rewards" (Würtemberg Confession, Article VII).[4] Others, then, speak as our fathers did, and we take their speech to have a sound meaning. So we may, and indeed ought to, take our fathers' speech in a sound sense, inasmuch as their meaning is doubtful, and charity always interprets doubtful things favorably. What should compel us to think that the punishment for the worst interpretation fell upon them all, rather than that the blessing of the better was granted to thousands?

Fifth, even if all had embraced the worst interpretation while living, might not many of them have utterly renounced it at death? However men, when they sit at ease, might tickle their hearts with some vain imagination of a correspondence between their merits and their rewards (which, in their mad speculations, they dream that God has measured, weighed, and laid up, as if in bundles for them), experience tells us that, when the hour of death approaches,

---

[4] Württemberg Confession, Article VII *De bonis operibus* (Of Good Works). This confession is a Lutheran document originally put together for delivery at the Council of Trent. The Latin quote Hooker is translating is as follows: *Docemus bona opera divinitus praecepta, necessario facienda esse, et mereri gratuita Dei clementia sua quaedam, siue corporalia, siue spiritualia, praemia* (499). For the Latin version of this confession, see *Die confessio Würtembergica*, in *Die Bekenntnisschriften Der Altprotestantischen Kirche Deutschlands*, ed. Heinrich Heppe (Cassel, 1855), 491–554.

and they secretly hear the summons to present themselves at the bar of that Judge whose brightness dazzles the eyes of the angels, all those idle imaginings begin to hide their faces. To list their merits *then* is to lay their souls upon the rack; the memory of their own deeds is loathsome to them; they forsake all things in which they have put any trust or confidence. No staff to lean upon, no ease, no rest, no comfort then, except for Christ Jesus.

22. Therefore, if the proposition were true that "to hold, as does the Church of Rome, that we cannot be saved by Christ alone—without works—is directly to deny the foundation of faith," I have nevertheless shown many ways that we may hope that thousands of our fathers who lived in popish superstitions might be saved. But what if this proposition is not true? What if neither the position of the Galatians concerning circumcision nor that of the Church of Rome concerning works is in fact any direct denial of the foundation, in the way my opponents affirm?

Strictly speaking, I do not need to wade into this controversy any further, inasmuch as the issue which first provoked concern is fully clarified, or so I would hope. However, because I desire to illuminate the truth in this matter, I will attempt to outline more plainly, *first*, what the foundation of faith is; *second*, what it means to directly deny the foundation; *third*, whether those whom God has chosen to be heirs of life may fall so far as to directly deny it; *fourth*, whether the Galatians did so by allowing the error about circumcision and the Law; and *last of all*, whether the Church of Rome, for its teaching on works, may be thought to have done likewise, and become no more a Christian church than the assemblies of Turks or Jews.

III:
WHAT IS THE FOUNDATION OF FAITH?

23. THIS WORD "foundation," in figurative usage, always refers to something resembling a physical building, both in Christian doctrine and within Christian community. Among the masters of civil policy nothing is more common than the insistence that commonwealths are founded upon laws, because a multitude cannot be united into one body except by a common acceptance of laws by which they are kept in order. The ground of all civil laws is this: "No man ought to be hurt or injured by another." Take away this persuasion, and you take away all laws; take away laws, and what shall become of commonwealths? So it is in our spiritual Christian community. I am not now referring to that mystical body of which Christ is the only head, that building which cannot be discerned by mortal eyes and of which Christ is the chief cornerstone. I am speaking of the visible Church, the foundation of which is the doctrine professed by the Prophets and Apostles. The point at which their doctrine aims is summarized in those words of Peter to Christ, "Thou hast the words of eternal life" (Jn. 6:68) and in those of Paul to Timothy: "The holy Scriptures are able to make thee wise unto salvation" (2 Tim. 3:15).

III

It is the demand of nature itself: "What shall we do to have eternal life?" (Jn. 6:68). The desire for immortality, and for the knowledge of how to obtain it, is so natural to all men that even those who are not persuaded that they will, still wish that they could know a way by which they might see no end to life. And because natural means are still unable to resist the force of death, there is no people on earth so savage which has not devised some supernatural help or other to which they might fly for aid and comfort in times of extremity against the enemies of their lives. So it is that, a longing to be saved, without an understanding of the true way of salvation, has been the cause of all the superstitions in the world. O that the miserable state of others, who wander in darkness without knowing where they are going, could give us understanding hearts able to worthily esteem the riches of the mercies of God toward us, before whose eyes the doors of the kingdom of heaven are thrown wide open! Should we not pursue the kingdom violently (Mt. 11:12)? It offers violence to us, and we gather strength to withstand it.

But I am wandering from my point when I lament the cold affections we have towards our salvation. My purpose here is rather to define what the ground of salvation is. The doctrine of the Gospel sets forth salvation as the end; doesn't it also teach the way by which salvation is attained? Yes, the young girl possessed by a spirit of divination spoke the truth, "These men are the servants of the Most High God who proclaim unto you the way of salvation" (Acts 16:17). "By the way which [Christ] dedicated for us, a new and living way, through the veil, that is to say, his flesh" (Heb. 10:20). Salvation is purchased by the death of Christ. By this foundation, before the time of the written Law, the children of God were distinguished from the sons of men. The revered patriarchs professed it while they were alive and spoke expressly of it at the hour of their death (Heb. 11:4–22). It comforted Job in the midst of his grief (Job 19:23–27). Later, it was the anchor for all of the righteous in Israel, from the writing of the Law until the time of grace; every Prophet makes mention of it (Lk. 1:70, 24:25–47). It was so famously spoken of that, when the coming of Christ to accomplish the promises made long before drew near, news of it was even heard among the Gentiles (Mt. 2:1–2).

When he came, as many as were his acknowledged that he was their salvation—he, that long-expected hope of Israel; he, that "seed in whom all the nations of the earth be blessed!" (Gen. 22:18; Gal. 3:16). Therefore, his name is now a name of ruin, a name of death and condemnation to those who dream of a new Messiah, to all who look for salvation by anyone other than him: "Neither is there any other name under heaven, that is given among men, wherein we must be saved" (Acts 4:12). St. Mark intimates as much at the outset of his book, opening with these words: "The beginning of the Gospel of Jesus Christ, the Son of God" (Mk. 1:1). He calls his doctrine the Gospel because it teaches salvation; it is the Gospel of Jesus Christ, the Son of God, because it teaches salvation by him. This, then, is the foundation upon which the structure of the Gospel is erected: that very Jesus—whom the Virgin conceived by the Holy Spirit, whom Simeon embraced in his arms (Lk. 2:28), whom Pilate condemned, whom the Jews crucified, whom the Apostles preached—he is Christ the Lord, the only Savior of the world: "other foundation no man can lay" (1 Cor. 3:11).

III

So then, I have briefly explained that principle in Christianity which we call the foundation of our faith. Now it follows that I should declare to you what it is to directly overthrow it. This will be better understood if we first understand what it is to hold the foundation of faith.

24. There are some who defend the idea that many of the Gentiles who have never heard the name of Christ hold the foundation of Christianity. Why? We know that many of them acknowledged the providence of God, his infinite wisdom, strength, and power, his goodness and his mercy toward the children of men; they knew that God has judgment in store for the wicked, but rewards for the righteous who seek him (Rom. 2:6–8, Heb. 11:6). In this confession of theirs, it is argued, Christian belief lies concealed; in their rudimentary knowledge of God, the foundation of our faith concerning Christ lies secretly wrapped up and is virtually contained. Therefore, they hold the foundation of our faith, although they have never heard of it. But might we not just as reasonably defend the idea that every ploughman has all the same knowledge in which philosophers excel? For no man is ignorant of the first principles which contain virtually whatever is known, or can be known, by natural means. Indeed, might we not with as much good reason affirm that a man plants three mighty oaks wherever three acorns are planted? For an acorn is an oak in potentiality.

25. To avoid such paradoxes, we plainly teach that to hold the foundation is to acknowledge it in express terms. Now, because the foundation is an affirmative proposition, all who deny it overthrow it; those who deny it directly overthrow it directly; and those who assert anything which would logically result in its denial can be said to overthrow

it indirectly or by consequence. What is the question separating the Gentiles and us, but this: is salvation by Christ? What is the question separating the Jews and us, but this: is salvation by this Jesus, whom we call Christ—yes or no? This is the main point on which Christianity stands, as is made clear by that one sentence of Festus concerning Paul's accusers: "They brought no charge or such evil things as I supposed; but had certain questions against him of their own religion, and one of Jesus, who was dead, whom Paul affirmed to be alive" (Acts 25:18–19). Here we see that Jesus, dead and raised for the salvation of the world, is denied by Jews, despised by a Gentile, and defended by a Christian apostle.

Therefore, the Fathers of the primitive Church defended Christianity in their writings against those who directly denied the foundation: Tertullian in the *Apologeticus*,[1] Minutius Felix in *Octavius*,[2] Arnobius in his seven books against the Gentiles,[3] Chrysostom in his orations against the

---

[1] Tertullian was a leading theologian of the Western church in the second and early third century. The *Apologeticus* is a plea for Christianity to be seen as legitimate in the eyes of the Roman empire.

[2] Marcus Minucius Felix (notice the difference in spelling) was an early-third-century apologist. *Octavius* is the only work attributed to him with confidence.

[3] Arnobius of Sicca was a fourth-century apologist. His most well-known work is the one cited here, *The Case against the Pagans*. For an English translation of this work along with an introduction, see Arnobius of Sicca, *The Case against the Pagans*, trans. George E. McCracken, 2 vols., Ancient Christian Writers 7 (New York, NY: Newman Press, 1949).

III

Jews,⁴ and Eusebius in his ten books of evangelical demonstration.⁵ But the writings of the Fathers against the Novatians,⁶ Pelagians,⁷ and other heretics of the like refute positions which only overthrow the foundation of Christian faith by consequence. In the former writings the foundation is proved; in the latter it is asserted as a proof, which to men

---

⁴ John Chrysostom was an important Eastern theologian from the fourth century. Chrysostom is well-known for his preaching and is remembered through his many written works. *Against the Jews* is a collection of homilies confronting Christians who continued to observe Jewish practices. For an English translation of this work along with an introduction, see John Chrysostom, *Discourses against Judaizing Christians*, trans. Paul W. Harkins, The Fathers of the Church: A New Translation 68 (1979; repr. Washington, D.C.: The Catholic University of America Press, 1999).

⁵ Eusebius of Caesarea was a famous early church historian and writer. He was Greek and lived from the middle of the third century to the middle of the fourth. Perhaps his most well known writing is his *Ecclesiastical History*. The work Hooker refers to here is his *Demonstratio evangelica*. Although this work was initially a collection of twenty books, only ten full books remain. For an English translation of this work, see Eusebius, *The Proof of the Gospel*, ed. and trans W. J. Ferrar, 2 vols. (Eugene, OR: Wipf and Stock, 2001).

⁶ The Novatians were a group that followed the teaching of Novatian, a third-century theologian. The Novatians denied fellowship in the Church to those who discredited their faith in response to the persecution of Decius. Even if the lapsed repented, the Novatians did not believe that they could return to the Church. However, Novatianism was denounced, as the Church sided instead with those who believed that the lapsed could be restored following repentance.

⁷ Pelagianism is a theological view named after the fourth-century monk Pelagius. Pelagianism was condemned in a council in 417. Most notably, Pelagianism is known for denying the Augustinian notion of original sin and for purporting that an individual can live one's entire life without sinning.

who had been known to directly deny the foundation must have seemed a worthless form of argument.

Therefore, all unbelievers directly deny the foundation of faith. But by consequence, many a Christian man, indeed whole Christian churches, have denied it, and deny it to the present day. How can this be—Christian churches denying the foundation of Christianity? They do so not directly, for then they would cease to be Christian churches; but they do so by consequence. In this regard we condemn them as erroneous, although inasmuch as they hold the foundation, we do and must consider them to be Christian.

IV:
CAN THE ELECT DENY THE FOUNDATION OF FAITH?

26. SO WE have seen what it is to hold the foundation, and what it is to deny it directly or by consequence. The next thing which follows is to ask whether they whom God has chosen to obtain the glory of our Lord Jesus Christ may, having once been effectually called and truly justified through faith, afterwards fall so far as directly to deny the foundation which their hearts have embraced with joy and comfort by the Holy Spirit, for such is the faith which truly justifies. Devils know the same things which we believe (James 2:19), and the minds of the most ungodly may be fully persuaded of the truth (John 8:12–59). Such knowledge in the one and persuasion in the other is sometimes termed faith, but equivocally, because it is not the sort of faith as that by which a Christian man is justified. It is the Spirit of adoption, who works faith in us, but not in them. The things which we believe, we understand by us not only as true, but also as good, and as good for us. Devils and the ungodly fail to apprehend them as good, but merely as true.

Here, then, there follows a third difference: the more the Christian man increases his faith, the more his joy and comfort abound; but they, the more sure they are of the truth, the more they quake and tremble at it. This begets another effect, in which the hearts of the one sort have a different disposition from the other. *Non ignoro plerosque conscientia meritorum, nihil se esse post mortem magis optare quam credere; malunt enim exstingui penitus, quam ad supplicia reparari.* "I am not ignorant," says Minutius, "that there are too many who, being conscious of what they are to look for, wish that they might, rather than think that they shall, cease to exist at all when they cease to live; they believe that it is better that death should totally consume them than that God should receive them for punishment."[1]

It is the same with the other articles of faith, which wicked men often think, no doubt, are altogether too true. On the other hand, to believers, there is no greater grief or torment than to feel themselves weakly persuaded of things from which, when they are strongly persuaded, they reap such comfort and joy of spirit. Such is the quality of the faith by which we are justified. As far as its object, faith neither justifies, nor is it faith, any longer than it holds that foundation of which we have spoken. It ceases to be faith when it ceases to believe that Jesus Christ is the only Savior of the world.

Now the cause of spiritual life in us is Christ—not carnally or corporately inhabiting us, but dwelling in the soul of man as something which (when the mind lays hold of it) is said to inhabit and possess the mind. The mind conceives of Christ by hearing the doctrine of Christianity. As the light of nature causes the mind to apprehend those truths which are merely rational, so that saving truth (which is far above the reach of human reason) cannot be conceived of other

---

[1] Marcus Minucius Felix, *Octavius* 34.52 (PL 3:0348A).

IV

than by the Spirit of the Almighty. All of the following are implied whenever any one of them is mentioned as the cause of spiritual life: when we read that "the Spirit is life" (Rom. 8:10) or "the Word of life" (Phil. 2:16, 1 Jn. 1:1) or "Christ, who is our life" (Col. 3:4), we are to understand in every case that our life is in Christ, who by the hearing of the Gospel is apprehended as a Savior, and assented to by the power of the Holy Ghost.

Embracing the concept and understanding of Christ in such a way is what St. Peter calls being "begotten again, not of corruptible seed, but of incoruptible" (1 Pet. 1:23). Our first embracing of Christ is our first reviving from the state of death and condemnation (Eph. 2:5). "He that hath the Son hath the life," says St. John, "and he that hath not the Son of God hath not the life" (1 Jn. 5:12). Therefore, if he who once has the Son ceases to have the Son, though it be but for a moment, he ceases for that moment to have life. But the life of those that live by the Son of God is everlasting; this life is not only everlasting in the world to come, but also because as "Christ being raised from the dead dieth no more; death no more hath dominion over him" (Rom. 6:9). So the justified man, being alive to God in Jesus Christ our Lord, by whom he has life, lives always (Rom. 6:11).

I might, if I had not already done so at length elsewhere,[2] show by various manifest and clear proofs how the

---

[2] Hooker is referring here to his sermon "A Learned and Comfortable Sermon of the Certainty and Perpetuity of Faith in the Elect. Especially of the Prophet Habakkuk's Faith." This sermon can be found in *The Works of that Learned and Judicious Divine Mr. Richard Hooker with an Account of His Life and Death by Isaac Walton*, ed. John Keeble, 7th ed., revised by R. W. Church and F. Paget, vol. 3 (Oxford: Clarendon Press, 1888), 469–81.

motions and operations of life are sometimes so indiscernible and secret that those who seem to be stone-dead, nonetheless, are still alive to God in Christ.

For as long as that which animates, quickens, and gives life abides in us, so long do we live; and we know that the cause of our life abides in us forever! If Christ, the fountain of life, may flit about and leave the habitation in which he once dwelt, what shall become of his promise, "I am with you always, even unto the end of the world" (Mt. 28:20)? If the seed of God, which contains Christ, may first be conceived and then be cast out, how can St. Peter term it immortal (1 Pet. 1:23)? How can St. John affirm that it abides (1 Jn. 3:9)? If the Spirit, which is given to cherish and preserve the seed of life, may be given and taken away, how is it the guarantee of our inheritance until the day of redemption (Eph. 1:14)? How then can it be said that the Spirit continues with us forever (Jn. 14:17)? If therefore the man who is once justified by faith shall live by faith and live forever, it follows that he who once believes the foundation must necessarily believe the foundation forever. If he believes it forever, how can he ever directly deny it? If faith holds the direct affirmation of the foundation, the direct negation is excluded, as long as faith continues.

But you will say that, just as he who is holy today, may forsake his holiness and become impure tomorrow, and as a friend may change his mind and become an enemy, and as hope may wither, so faith may die in the heart of a man, the Spirit may be quenched, grace may be extinguished, and those who believe may be quite turned away from the truth. The case seems clear, long experience has made this manifest—this requires, it seems, no proof.

IV

I grant that we are apt, prone, and ready to forsake God. But is God ready to forsake us? Our minds are changeable—is his likewise? Has not Christ assured those whom God has justified that it is his Father's will to give them a kingdom (Lk. 12:32)? Note that this kingdom shall not be given to them unless they "continue in the faith, grounded and steadfast, and not moved from the hope of the gospel" (Col. 1:23), and "if they continue in faith and love and sanctification" (1 Tim. 2:15). Therefore, when our Savior said of the sheep effectually called and truly gathered into his fold, "I give unto them eternal life; and they shall never perish, and no one shall snatch them out of my hand" (Jn. 10:28), in so promising to save them, he promised without doubt to preserve them in that faith without which there can be no salvation, as well as from that by which salvation is irremediably lost.

Every error in things relating to God is repugnant to faith; every fearful thought to hope; to love, every straggling, inordinate desire; to holiness, every blemish by which either the inner thoughts of our minds or the outer actions of our lives are stained.

But heresy such as that of Ebion,[3] Cerinthus,[4] and others, whom the Apostles were forced to oppose by word and by writing; or that complaining discouragement of heart

---

[3] The Ebionites were a group in the early Church who are most well known for holding a deviant Christology. They denied the virgin birth and believed Jesus was born as a result of sexual intercourse between Mary and Joseph. The Ebionites thus denied the full divinity of Jesus Christ.

[4] Cerinthus was a first-century Gnostic writer. Cerinthus and the Ebionites held the same Christological error—namely, that Jesus was not born of a virgin and that he was not fully God.

which tempts God, of which Israel in the desert are an example; or coldness like that described by the angel of Ephesus (Rev. 2:4–7); or foul sins known to be expressly against the first or second table of the Law such as Noah, Manasseh, David, Solomon, and Peter committed: these are each in their kind so opposed to the virtues listed above that they leave no place for salvation without actual repentance.

But infidelity, extreme despair, hatred of God and all godliness, stubbornness in sin, cannot stand where there is the least spark of faith, hope, love, or sanctity, just as cold of the lowest degree cannot exist where heat of any degree is found.

Therefore, I conclude that although in the first way listed above, there is no man alive who does not sin, and in the second way, even the most perfect man alive may sin—yet since the man who is born of God has a promise that the seed of God shall "abideth in him" (1 Jn. 3:9)—this seed is a sure preservative against the sins of the third kind. We cannot have any greater and clearer assurance than this: that God shall preserve the righteous, the apple of his eye, from such sins forever. To directly deny the foundation of faith is plain infidelity; but wherever faith has entered a life, infidelity is excluded forever. Therefore, the foundation of Christian faith can never be directly denied by anyone who has once sincerely believed in Christ. But did not Peter, did not Marcellinus,[5] did not many others, both directly deny Christ after they had believed, and then again believe after

---

[5] Marcellinus was a Pope from 296–304 who, according to some accounts, sacrificed to pagan gods during the time of the Diocletian persecution. According to these accounts, he then later repented of his actions and sought out martyrdom.

IV

they had denied him? No doubt; for just as some may confess in word whose condemnation, nevertheless, is their not believing in heart (an example is Judas), some may believe in heart, whose condemnation (apart from repentance) is their not confessing in word. Thus, although Peter and the rest (for whose faith Christ had prayed that their faith might not fail) did not commit by their denial the sin of infidelity, which is an inward renunciation of Christ (for if they had done this, their faith would have clearly failed), it was necessary that God, whose purpose it was to save their souls, should touch their hearts with genuine repentance so that his mercy might restore again to life those whose sin had made them the children of death and condemnation, because they sinned notoriously and grievously, committing that which they knew to be so expressly forbidden by the Law—which says, "Thou shalt fear Jehovah thy God; and him shalt thou serve" (Dt. 6:13).

Therefore, I hope I can safely say that if the one who is justified errs, as he may, and never comes to understand his error, God will save him through general repentance; if he falls into heresy, God will recall him at one time or another by actual repentance; but from infidelity, which is an inward and direct denial of the foundation, God will preserve him by special providence forever.

With this in mind, we may easily know what to think of those Galatians, whose hearts were so possessed with love for the truth, that, if it had been possible, they would have plucked out their very eyes to bestow on their teachers (Gal. 4:15). It is true that afterwards they were greatly changed, both in convictions and affection, so much so that when St. Paul wrote to them, they were not the Galatians which they had been in former times, because they wandered through error although they were still his sheep (Gal. 1:6). I do not deny this, but if I should grant that they had perished through error, I would be denying that they were his sheep. In those who held it only as an error, it was a perilous opinion, because as a matter of consequence it overthrows the foundation of faith. But in the case of those who obstinately maintained it, I cannot think it less than a damnable heresy.

Therefore, we must draw a distinction between those who err out of ignorance, nevertheless retaining a mind desirous to be instructed in the truth, and those who, after the truth is plainly laid out, persist in stubborn defense of their blindness. The blessed Apostle calls willful and stiff-necked heretics, defenders of circumcision, "dogs" (Phil. 3:2). But foolish men, who were seduced to think they taught the truth, he pities, takes them up in his arms, lovingly embraces, and kisses. With more tenderness than a father, he tempers, qualifies, and adjusts his speech toward them to such an extent that a man cannot easily discern which was most abundant—the love which he had for their godly affection, or the grief which came from the danger of their belief. Their belief was dangerous, of course. But was that not also the case for those who thought that the kingdom of Christ should be earthly? Was that not the case for those who thought that the Gospel should only be preached to the Jews? What is more contrary to prophetic doctrine concerning the coming of Christ than the first of these, and what more contrary to the catholic Church, than the other? Yet those who had these fancies, even when they held them, were not the worst men in the world. The heresy of "free will" was a millstone around the Pelagians' neck. Shall we, therefore, inevitably give the sentence of death to all those Fathers in the ancient Greek church, who, being wrongly persuaded, died in the error of free will?

Concerning those Galatians, therefore, who first were justified and then later deceived: since I can see no cause why all those who died uncorrected might not be saved by mercy even in their error, so I have no doubt that all who lived until they *were* corrected found the mercy of God effectual in converting them from their error, so that none who are Christ's should perish. On this point, I take it, there is no controversy. However if there is controversy, it only concerns the salvation of those who died before correction, while still in error; it is objected that their opinion was a very plain direct denial of the foundation of faith. But if Paul and Barnabas had thought so, they would have surely used different terms when speaking of the very teachers who first broached the error as "a certain sect of the Pharisees who believed" (Acts 15:5). What difference was there between these Pharisees and others, from whom they are distinguished by a special description, but this: that those who came to Antioch, teaching the necessity of circumcision, were Christians; the others were enemies of Christianity. Why then should these be so distinctly called "believers," if they directly denied the foundation of our belief, when apart from this there was nothing else which made the rest to be "unbelievers"?

To prove this point, we need go no farther than St. Paul's own reasoning against them: "But now that ye have come to know God, or rather to be known by God, how turn ye back again to the weak and beggarly rudiments?" (Gal. 4:9). The Law creates servants, her children are in bondage. They who are begotten by the Gospel are free.

"Brethren, we are not children of the handmaid, but of the free woman" (Gal. 4:31). They thought that it was necessary for the salvation of the Church of Christ to observe days, months, times, and years and to keep the ceremonies and the sacraments of the Law (Gal. 4:10). This was their error. Yet he who condemned their error confessed nonetheless that they knew God and were known by him. He did not take from them the honor of being termed sons begotten by the immortal seed of the Gospel. Let his harshest words be weighed; consider the meaning of those dreadful conclusions: "If ye receive circumcision, Christ shall profit ye nothing; ye who would be justified by the law, ye are fallen from grace" (Gal. 5:2, 4). There would have been no point in thus urging them had not the Apostle been persuaded that in hearing of such consequences—"Christ shall profit ye nothing," "fallen from grace"—their hearts would tremble and quake within them. And why? Because the Galatians knew that their salvation lay in Christ, in grace—a direct acknowledgment of the foundation.

If by saying this, I should seem to go beyond what other godly and learned persons have said, consider these words of Martin Bucer, which imply the same things which I have affirmed:

> Surely those brothers, who in St. Paul's time thought that God laid a necessity upon them to make a choice of days and meats, spoke as they believed, and could not do otherwise than condemn such a "freedom" which they supposed to have been brought in against the authority of divine Scripture. Otherwise it would have been needless for St. Paul to admonish

IV

them not to condemn those who ate without scrupulosity whatever was set before them. This error, if you consider what it is in and of itself, served to overthrow all of the Scriptures, by which we are taught salvation by faith in Christ; all that the prophets ever foretold, all that the apostles preached of Christ. It brought with it a denial of Christ entirely, so much so that St. Paul complains that his labor for the Galatians—upon whom this error was forced—has been in vain (Gal. 4:10–11); St. Paul responds by stating that if they were circumcised, Christ should not profit them anything at all.

Yet St. Paul was so far from erasing their names out of Christ's book of life that he commanded others to entertain them, to accept them with singular humanity, to treat them like brothers. He knew man's imbecility; he had a feeling for our blindness, we mortal men, how great it is. And yet being sure that whoever God endowed with his fear were the sons of God, he would not have them be counted as enemies of that which they could not yet conceive themselves to be friends, who even out of a very religious affection for the truth, unwittingly rejected and resisted the truth! They acknowledged Christ to be their only and their perfect Savior, but did not see how repugnant their believing in the necessity of Mosaic ceremonies was to their faith in Jesus Christ (Martin Bucer, *De unitate ecclesia servanda*).[6]

To this, some will reply that if they had not directly denied the foundation, they might have been saved; but they could not in fact be saved, so their opinion must have been not only an implicit denial of the foundation, but a direct denial. When we were discussing the possibility of their salvation, their denial of the foundation was given as proof that they could not be saved. Now that the question concerns their denial, the impossibility of their salvation is given as proof that they denied the foundation! Is there nothing which excludes men from salvation but the denial of the foundation of the faith? I should have thought that besides this, many other things are spiritual death, unless actually repented of. Indeed, this opinion of theirs was fatal to anyone who understood that to cleave to it was to fall away from Christ and still nonetheless cleaved to it. But enough of this!

Therefore, I come to the last question: whether the doctrine of the Church of Rome concerning the necessity of works to salvation is a direct denial of the foundation of our faith.

---

[6] Martin Bucer (1491–1551) was a highly influential first-generation Reformer. He was a German who served in Strasbourg and served for a brief period in England. Although Hooker references him here, the exact work he is referring to is unknown. The title given, *De unitate ecclesia servanda*, does not describe any of his works exactly. It may refer to his work *Enarrationes perpetuae, in sacra quatuor Evangelia*, but there is no obvious connection with the cited passage.

V:
DOES ROME DIRECTLY DENY THE FOUNDATION OF FAITH?

27. I AM seeking to not force upon you any private opinions of my own. The most learned in our profession share this judgment: that all the heresies and corruptions of the Church of Rome do not prove her to deny the foundation directly. If such corruptions did, they would prove her simply to be no Christian church at all. "But I suppose," says one, "that in the papacy some church remains, a church crazed, or, if you will, broken quite in pieces, forlorn, misshapen, yet some church" (Calvin, *Letter 104*, ca. 1549). His reason is this: "*Antichrist must sit in the temple of God*" (2 Thes. 2:3–4).[1] Some may think sentences like this to be true only of those whom, by the special providence of God, that church is supposed to have kept free from infection in the secret corner of his bosom, and as sound in the faith as, we trust by his mercy we ourselves are. However, I propose for

---

[1] John Calvin, Letter to Lelio Socino, December 9, 1549. Unfortunately, this letter does not seem to be among those that have been translated into English. For the Latin text, see Joannis Calvini, *Epistolae 1323: Calvinus Socino*, in *Opera quae supersunt omnia*, ed. Guilielmus Baum, Eduardus Cunitz, and Eduardus Reuss, vol. 13 (Brunsvigae: C. A. Schwetschke Et Filium, 1875), 484–87.

your wise consideration whether it might not be more likely that, just as madness takes away the use of reason but yet still proves madmen to be reasonable creatures (because none can be mad but those who are capable of reason), so Anti-Christianity, being the bane and contradiction of Christianity, may nevertheless prove that the church where Antichrist is seated is Christian. Regarding this point, I have never heard or read a single word that can prove that God does anything other than (as we have seen in considering the previous two questions) bind himself to keep his elect from worshiping the Beast or from receiving his mark on their foreheads (Rev. 13:16, 14:9). He has preserved and will preserve them from receiving any deadly wound at the hands of the Man of Sin, whose deceit has prevailed over none to the point of death, except for those who never loved the truth and who took pleasure in unrighteousness. Those of every age whose hearts have delighted in the essential truths of the faith, and whose souls have thirsted after righteousness, if they later received the mark of error—even dangerous error—the mercy of God might save them; if they received the mark of heresy, the same mercy, I have no doubt, converted them.

The question here is not to what extent Roman heresies might prevail over God's elect, and how many have been converted from them; for even if heaven had not received anyone of the Roman Catholic profession over the last thousand years, it could still be true that the doctrine which they profess to this day does not directly deny the foundation or prove that they are not a Christian church. I have already quoted one theologian whose words, in my ears, sound that way. Shall I add another whose words are even more plain? "I do not deny her the name of a 'church,'" says another, "no more than I would deny the name of a 'man' to a man as long as he lives, whatever sickness he has" (Philip Mornay du Plessis, ca. 1577). His reason is this: "Salvation in Jesus Christ—which is the mark that joins the Head with the body, Jesus Christ with His Church—is so severed by man's merits, by the merits of the saints, by the Pope's pardons, and such other wickedness, that the life of the Church holds by only a very little thread," yet still the life of the Church holds.[2]

A third theologian's words are these: "I acknowledge the Church of Rome, even at this present day, to be a church of Christ; a church as Israel was under Jeroboam, yet a church." His reason is this:

> Every man sees, unless he willingly hoodwinks himself, that as always and so now, the Church of Rome holds firmly and steadfastly to the doctrine of truth concerning God and the Person of our Lord Jesus Christ, baptizes in the name of the Father, the Son, and the Holy Spirit, confesses and vouches for Christ as the only Redeemer of the world and the Judge that shall pass judgment upon the living and the

---

[2] Philip Mornay Du Plessis (1549–1623), usually known as Du-Plessis-Mornay or Mornay Du Plessis, was a French Protestant writer and member of the anti-monarchist Monarchomaques. He spent time in the court of Elizabeth I, and befriended English Protestants such as Francis Walsingham and Philip Sydney. He was chosen to represent French Protestants at Dort in 1618, but could only contribute in writing after being prevented from attending by King Louis XIII. He was also instrumental in writing the 1598 Edict of Nantes, securing religious freedoms for French Huguenots. For the section cited here, see Philip of Mornay, *A Treatise of the Church* (London: Christopher Barker, 1581), ch. 2., pp. 38–39, 44–45.

dead, receiving true believers into endless joy, and casting faithless and godless men with Satan and his angels into flames unquenchable (Jerome Zanchi).[3]

28. I will focus the controversy more sharply than my opponents. Let the Pope take off his crown, and no longer take men's souls captive by his papal jurisdiction. Let him no longer consider himself to be lord paramount over the princes of the earth, and no longer hold kings as his tenants *paravail*.[4] Let his stately senate submit their necks to the yoke of Christ, and cease to dye their garments, like Edom, in blood. Let them, from the highest to the lowest, hate and forsake their idolatry, recant all their errors and heresies by which they have perverted the truth. Let them cleanse their church, leaving no polluted rag, except for this banner around her: "We cannot be saved by Christ alone without works!" It is enough for me if I show that the holding of this one thing does not prove that the Church of Rome directly denies the foundation of faith.

29. Works are an addition to the foundation. That being so, what of it? The foundation is not subverted by *every* kind of addition. To simply add to those fundamental truths

---

[3] Girolamo ("Jerome") Zanchi (1516–1590) was an Italian Protestant who is known for being a mentee of Peter Martyr Vermigli. Zanchi followed in the philosophical tradition from Padua and is an important figure in Protestant Scholasticism. The section here is from *De religione Christiana fides, Epistola ad Ulyssem Martinengum* (Letter to Ulysses Martinengus). For a scholarly edition to this work, see Girolamo Zanchi, *De religione Christiana fides (Confession of Christian Religion)*, ed. Luca Baschera and Christian Moser, Studies in the History of Christian Traditions 135 (Leiden: Brill, 2007). For this section in particular, see p. 56.

[4] That is, the lowest level of tenant, who rents the land of another tenant.

is not to mingle wine with water, heaven with earth, polluted things with the sanctified blood of Christ. By all means, accuse of such a crime anyone who attributes, in whole or in part, to any creature those operations which, in the work of our salvation, belong wholly to Christ. If I open my mouth to speak in their defense, or if I hold my peace and fail to plead against them as long as breath is in my body, let me be guilty of all the dishonor that has ever been done to the Son of God.

But, given how dreadful a thing it is to deny salvation by Christ alone, I am all the more slow and fearful to accuse any man of such without manifest proof. Let us beware, lest we make so many ways of denying Christ, that we scarcely leave any way for ourselves to truly and soundly confess him! Salvation by Christ alone is indeed the true foundation upon which Christianity stands. But what if I say that you cannot be saved by Christ alone without this addition: Christ must be believed upon in the heart, confessed with the mouth, and obeyed in life and conversation? Because I add this, do I therefore deny that which I did directly affirm?

One may attach to any proposition an added clarification which does not overthrow it, but rather proves and concludes it. For example, to say that "Peter was a chief Apostle" proves that Peter was an Apostle (Gal. 2:9). Or to say that that our salvation is of the Lord, "in sanctification of the Spirit and belief of the truth," proves that our salvation is of the Lord (2 Thes. 2:13). But if that which is added qualifies the original statement so much that it takes away its very essence, then it overthrows it by logical consequence. And so, to say, "Our election is of grace for our works' sake," appears to say that our election is of grace, but denies this by necessary consequence of the qualification;

for the grace which elects us is no grace at all if it elects us for our works' sake.[5]

30. Now, while we agree that the Church of Rome adds works, we must note that the adding of works to Christ is not like the adding of circumcision. Christ did not come to repeal or do away with good works; he did, however, come to change circumcision, for we see he substituted holy baptism in its place. To say "you cannot be saved by Christ unless you are circumcised" is to add a thing which has been excluded—that is, a thing which it is not only unnecessary to keep, but which it is in fact necessary *not* to keep by those who will be saved. On the other hand, to say "you cannot be saved by Christ without works" is to add things which are not only not excluded, but are in fact commanded. They have their place and are necessary in a certain respect, although they are subordinated to Christ by Christ himself, who spins the web of our salvation: "Except your righteousness shall exceed the righteousness of the scribes and Pharisees, ye shall in no wise enter the kingdom of heaven" (Mt. 5:20). The scribes and the Pharisees rigorously practiced things which were commanded, and so should not have been totally neglected and left undone, such as washings and tithings, etc. As they were in these lesser things, so we must

---

[5] Hooker is using a syllogism in reference to what seems to be Massilianism, most popularly known as "Semi-Pelagianism." Massilianism was a fifth-century movement that believed that grace is given to an individual in response to a person's faith, rather than the Augustinian view that grace is given in order that a person will have faith. For a look at Pelagianism and Massilianism and how Augustine and Prosper of Aquitaine responded to these views, see Jonathan N. Cleland, "Pelagianism, Massilianism, and the Development of the Doctrine of Sin," *Evangelical Quarterly* 92, no. 3 (November 2021): 246–59.

be in greater things such as right judgment and our love of God. Christ extends more liberty than the Pharisees with regard to ceremonial works, but with much less than they did with regard to moral works (Mt. 5:21–48). Therefore, adding works of righteousness to the proposition that "salvation is by Christ alone" is not as repugnant as adding circumcision to it.

31. But we often say that our salvation is by Christ alone and, therefore, so the objection goes, anything that we add to Christ in the matter of salvation overthrows him. But this position is very difficult to maintain if applied universally. For we do not teach Christ alone in such a way that excludes the necessity of faith for justification, or works for sanctification, or either as being unnecessary to salvation. Our adversaries greatly please themselves with a childish, petty objection, in regard to justification, when they argue that we tread all Christian virtues under our feet and require nothing of Christians but faith, simply because we teach that faith alone justifies. However, this teaching is never meant to exclude hope and love from always being inseparably joined with the faith of a justified person, nor to suggest that works are not a necessary obligation, required from all who are justified. Rather, we mean to show that faith is the only hand which can put on Christ for justification, and that Christ is the only garment which, once worn, covers the shame of our defiled natures, hides the imperfections of our works, and preserves us blameless in God's sight. Otherwise the very weakness of our faith would be sufficient cause to make us culpable before God, and to shut us out of the kingdom of heaven, into which nothing impure can enter!

If we are not to be as childish towards them as they are to us, we must take note of what precisely is excluded (and where) when we hear of salvation by Christ alone and consider "alone" as an exclusive participle. For example, if I say, "Only a certain kind of judge ought to determine a certain case," everything else relevant to the case's determination besides the judge (such as laws, depositions, evidence, etc.) is not thereby excluded. Certain people are of course excluded from judging and sentencing, but not from witnessing or assisting. Similarly, what do we mean when we say that our salvation is worked by Christ alone? Do we mean that nothing is requisite to man's salvation but for Christ to save, and man to be saved without anything more to do? No, we acknowledge no such foundation to our faith.

Rather, we teach what we received: that besides the bare and naked work in which Christ alone, without any other partner, accomplished every part of our redemption and purchased our salvation, many things are required for this eminent blessing to be conveyed to us. For example, we must be known and chosen by God before the foundation of the world; we must be called, justified, and sanctified in the world; after we have left the world we must be received into glory. Christ, in each stage, has something which he works alone. Through him—born, crucified, buried, raised, etc., and according to the eternal purpose of God before the foundation of the world—we were, by grace, known to God long before we were known to anyone else. God knew us, loved us, and was merciful toward us in Christ Jesus. In him we were elected to be heirs of life (Eph. 1:3ff.).

In what we've just outlined, God has worked through Christ alone in such a way that we are mere patients, working no more than dead and senseless matter—like wood, stone, or iron do in the craftsman's hand; no more than the clay when the potter appoints it for an honorable use. In fact, not even that much—the craftsman chooses the material upon which he works based upon how fit it is for his purposes; in us there is no such thing.

We can briefly consider the rest of God's work which makes up the foundation of our faith: that we are called by him, that we have redemption and remission of sins through his blood, health by his wounds, justice by him, that he sanctifies his Church and makes it glorious in his sight, that we are given entrance into joy by him. All of these are things which God does alone. However, these are not done by him alone as if any of the following were unnecessary: our hearing of the Gospel for our calling, faith for our justification, the fruits of the Spirit for our sanctification, perseverance in hope, faith, and holiness until our entrance into rest.

32. So what is the error of the Church of Rome? It is not that she requires works from those that would be saved, but that she attributes to works both the power to satisfy God's wrath against sin, and the ability to merit grace on earth and glory in heaven. I willingly grant that this *overthrows* the foundation of faith; however, I utterly deny that it is a *direct denial* of the foundation of faith. I have already stated both what it means to hold and to deny the foundation of faith, and if we apply that to the case of the Church of Rome there will be no more fuss. Whatever thing we consider, if the form by which it is considered is added to the thing, it makes apparent the foundation of any doctrine whatsoever. Christ is the subject matter with which the doctrine of the Gospel is concerned; and the Gospel treats Christ as a Savior. Therefore, salvation by Christ is the foundation of Christianity. Works are a subordinate thing, only necessary in that our sanctification cannot be accomplished without

them. The doctrine of works is something built upon the foundation of salvation by Christ.

Therefore, a doctrine of works which imagines that works have the power to atone for sin or to merit grace adds to something which is built upon the foundation, and thus subordinate or secondary to it; it does not add not to the very foundation itself. But does this addition overthrow the foundation by logical consequence? It would seem so, for we may state the following: anyone who states that good works acceptable in God's sight can proceed from the natural freedom of our will; anyone who gives to any good work of ours the power to satisfy God's wrath against sin or the power to merit earthly or heavenly rewards; anyone who believes that good works prior to our calling were given in congruity[6] to merit our calling, or that works following our first justification merit our second justification and, by condignity,[7] our last reward in the kingdom of heaven, pulls the doctrine of faith up by the roots. We could conclude the plain and direct denial of the foundation of faith from every one of these statements. Indeed, what heresy is there which, by consequence, doesn't ultimately demolish the very foundation of faith?

However, we do distinguish between heresies. Any which directly deny something which is expressly acknowledged in our articles of belief we regard as apostasy, since the denial of the very foundation can be immediately inferred from the denial of such clear and important articles. For example: if a man said, "There is no catholic Church," it follows immediately that Jesus, whom we call the Savior,

---

[6] "Congruity" being merit given undeservedly, prior to a state of grace, in order to bestow it.

[7] "Condignity" being merit earned whilst in a state of grace.

is not the Savior of the world, because all the Prophets testify that the true Messiah will be a light for the Gentiles (Is. 42:6, Acts 26:23); that is, he will gather such a Church that is truly catholic, and no longer restricted to one circumcised nation.

In a second category, we can place heresies containing positions from which the denial of any of our articles of belief may be logically inferred just as clearly as if they'd been explicitly denied. This encompasses those who have denied either the divinity of Christ, such as the Ebionites, or humanity, such as the Marcionites. We can see a clear example of such reasoning in the defense of the incarnation of the Son of God by Cassianus against Nestorius, Archbishop of Constantinople. Nestorius held that when the Virgin Mary gave birth to Christ, she did not give birth to the Son of God, but to a solitary, mere man.[8] From this heresy, Cassian deduced the denial of the following articles of the Christian faith:

> If you deny our Lord Jesus Christ to be
> God, then in denying the Son, you cannot

---

[8] Hooker mistakenly says "Archbishop of Antioch" when it should be "Archbishop of Constantinople," as we have it here. Hooker's definition of Nestorius's thought here also requires clarification. Most specifically, Nestorius denied the name *Theotokos* for Mary, a Greek word meaning "God-Bearer," suggesting instead the name *Christotokos*, meaning "Christ-Bearer." Although he put himself in conflict by challenging the term *Theotokos* for Mary, it is unclear whether or not he is to be attributed fully with the heresy named after him. For example, Hooker's accusation that Nestorius believed Christ was a "mere man" is denied by some scholars today. For a helpful and brief overview of Nestorius's view, see P. T. Camelot, "Nestorianism," in *New Catholic Encyclopedia*, 2nd ed., vol. 10 (Detroit, MI: Gale, 2003), 252–54.

but choose to deny the Father. For according to the voice of the Father himself, "He that hath not the Son hath not the Father." Therefore, in denying him that is begotten, you deny him who begets. Again, having denied the Son of God to have been born in the flesh, how can you believe that he suffered? Not believing in his passion, what remains but that you deny his resurrection? For we do not believe him to be raised, except that we first believe him to be dead. Neither can the reason for his rising from the dead stand, without prior faith in his death. The denial of his death and passion infers the denial of his rising from the depths. From there it follows that you also deny his ascension into heaven, for the Apostle affirms, "that he which ascended did first descend." So that, as much as lies in you, our Lord Jesus Christ has neither risen from the depths, nor is ascended into heaven, nor sits at the right hand of the Father, neither shall he come at the day of final account (for which we look), nor shall he judge the quick and dead! Dare you set your foot in the Church? Can you think of yourself as a bishop, when you deny all those things by which you obtained a bishoply calling? (John Cassian, *On the Incarnation of the Lord*, Chapter 17, ca. 430).[9]

---

[9] John Cassian (c. 360–425 AD) was a monk and theologian. His work *On the Incarnation of the Lord*, which is quoted here, was a direct refutation of the supposedly heterical Christology of Nestorius. For Hooker's quote here, see John Cassian, *De incarnatione Christi contra Nestorium* 6.17–18 (PL 50:0177A–0178B).

V

Although Nestorius confessed all the articles of the creed, his opinion necessarily implied the denial of every part of his confession!

Finally, there are heresies of a third sort, and these are the kind maintained by the Church of Rome. These are removed from the foundation by a greater distance. Although they do indeed overthrow the foundation, the contradictions between such heresy and the foundation are not so quickly nor so easily recognized, due to the weakness which the Philosopher detects in men's rational capacities (i.e., that the average person cannot understand things which logically follow only after many deductions).[10] Therefore, a heretic of this third kind, rather than of the former kind, may directly grant the foundation of faith and yet still deny it by logical consequence.

33. Now if my reasoning seems suspect, putting it to the test will show that the Church of Rome does exactly as I have said when she teaches her doctrine of works. Present them with the fundamental words "salvation is by Christ alone," and what one man is there who will refuse to subscribe to them? Can they directly grant, and directly deny one and the very same thing? Indeed, our own arguments against their doctrine of works assume that they not only hold to the foundation of the faith, but that we acknowledge them to do so in spite of their opinion. We make arguments such as "Christ alone has satisfied and appeased his Father's

---

[10] "The Philosopher" is Aristotle (384–22 BC). His preeminence among philosophers and theologians in the Middle Ages, and into the Reformation, earned him this title. The work Hooker is referring to here is *Rhetoric*. For an English translation, see Aristotle, *A New Translation of Aristotle's Rhetoric*, trans. John Gillies (London: T. Cadell, 1823). For the section referenced here, see Book I chapters 1–2, pp. 151–67.

wrath" and "Christ alone has merited salvation." We would be fools to make such arguments, or hope we could persuade someone with them, if we based them on a premise to which we know our opponents do not hold or consent. Their responses to all the arguments brought against them in this controversy make it abundantly clear that they hold to this foundation.

No one who has read their books on this matter can be ignorant as to how they develop their answers under the following premises:

1. The remission of all our sins, the pardon of all punishments we deserve, the rewards which God has laid up in heaven, are purchased by the blood of our Lord Jesus Christ, and are sufficient for all men, but efficient for no man in particular, unless the blood of Christ is applied to him in particular by such means as God has appointed for this work.

2. Those means are by themselves mere dead things, which only the blood of Christ enlivens, empowers, and makes efficacious, working in them, and being available, each in its kind, for our salvation.

3. Finally, grace is purchased for us by the blood of Christ, and is initially bestowed upon us freely without any merit or virtue deserving reward; by this means, the good things which we do after having received grace are made satisfactory and meritorious.

To prove this, consider these passages from their own theologians. Here is the judgment of one foreigner:

> He that would count how many are the virtues and merits of our Savior Jesus Christ might likewise understand how many are the benefits that have come to us by him,

because men are made partakers of all of them by the means of his passion. By him we are *given* remission of our sins, grace, glory, liberty, praise, peace, salvation, redemption, justification, justice, sanctification, sacraments, merits, doctrine, and all other things which he had and were necessary for our salvation (Lewis of Granada, *The Book of Prayer and Meditation*).[11]

In another Roman authority, we have this reply:

> All grace is given by Christ Jesus. True; but not without Christ Jesus being applied. He is the propitiation for our sins. By his stripes we are healed. He has offered up himself for us. All this is true, but it must be applied. We put all satisfaction in the blood of Jesus Christ; but we hold that the means which Christ has appointed for us to apply it in this case are our penal works (Francis Panigarola, *Letter 11*, ca. 1587).[12]

Our fellow Englishmen, the Roman "recusants" in Rheims, France, provide the same response: they seek salvation no

---

[11] Louis of Granada (1504–1588) was a Dominican friar, and a noted theologian, writer, and preacher. For the passage referred to here, see "Of the Passing great benefite of our Redemption," pt. 3 of The Last Chapter, in *Of Prayer and Meditation* (Rouen: George L'Oiselet, 1584), 664.

[12] Francesco Panigarola was a sixteenth-century Italian. He was a theologian and preacher and aimed to renounce doctrines of the Reformation. The work cited here is from a dispute against Calvinism. See F. Francisci Panigarolae, *Disceptatio ndecima* (Discussion Eleven), in *Ecclesiae hastensis Episcopi: Disceptationes Caluinicae* (Pacifici Pontij Impressoris Archiepisc, 1594), 272, 273. Unfortunately, this work does not seem to have been translated into English.

other way than by the blood of Christ.[13] And they humbly use prayer, fasting, alms, faith, charity, sacrifice, sacraments, and priests only as the *means* appointed by Christ to apply the benefit of his holy blood to them. They do not consider our good works meritorious or responsible for the joys of heaven according to their own nature. These joys come by the grace of Christ—not by our works, as if we have a right to heaven and are worthily deserving due to our good deeds.

If anyone thinks that I am trying to polish Roman opinions and to set the better foot of a lame cause forward, he should know that, since I began to thoroughly understand the Roman position, I have found their limping in this doctrine greater than it might at first appear to those who "know not the deep things of Satan," of which blessed St. John the Divine speaks (Rev. 2:24). For, although the testimonies above sufficiently prove that they do not *directly deny* the foundation of faith, it is still more than enough to prove that their doctrine *is not agreeable* with the foundation of Christian faith, even if this were the only leaven in the whole lump. After all, the Pelagians, too friendly to nature, made themselves enemies of grace even though they professed that men have their souls and natural faculties (i.e., their wills and the abilities of their wills) from God.

And is the Church of Rome not still an opponent of Christ's merits because she teaches that the blood of Christ gives us the power to merit God's favor? Sir Thomas More expresses the differences between us and the Church of Rome with regard to works as follows:

---

[13] "Recusants" were those Roman Catholics who refused to submit to the Church of England or to attend its services. Some fled to Catholic countries; others remained in England and suffered fines for non-attendance of services.

V

We grant them that no good work of man's own nature is deserving of reward in heaven, apart from the goodness of God who stoops to set so high a price upon so poor a thing; and that God settles this price through Christ's passion; and also that they are his own works with us, for no man does good works towards God without God working within him; and we grant them that no man may be proud of his own imperfect works; and that for all that man can do, he can do no good, but is merely an unprofitable servant who does bare duty.

As we grant them these things, so they also grant us one or two things in return: that men are bound to work good works, if they have time and ability; and that whoever works the most in true faith shall be most rewarded. But then they begin to assert that all a man's rewards shall be given to him for his faith alone, and nothing at all for his works, because they say that his faith is the thing that empowers him to work well (*A Dialogue of Comfort against Tribulation*, chapter 1, section 11, 1534).[14]

---

[14] Sir Thomas More (1478–1555) was an English lawyer, writer, and thinker, who served as Lord High Chancellor under Henry VIII. He was a fierce opponent of the Reformation and opposed Henry's departure from Rome. After refusing to swear the Oath of Supremacy which acknowledged Henry as Supreme Head of the Church of England, and refusing to acknowledge his annulment from Catherine of Aragon, More was executed. For the section cited here, see Sir Thomas More, *A Dialogue of Comfort against*

One can see from Thomas More, then, how easy it is for men of great capacity and judgment to misunderstand things written or spoken, on one side of an argument or the other.

Roman doctrine, so More thought, makes a man's works worthy of reward in the world to come through the mere goodness of God, who is pleased to set so high a price upon so poor a thing. And our Protestant doctrine, so More thought, is that a man receives that eternal and high reward, not for his works, but for his faith's sake, by which he then works. However, in reality, our doctrine is simply that which we have learned at the feet of Christ: that God justifies the believing man, not because of the worthiness of his belief, but because of the worthiness of him who is believed. God abundantly rewards everyone who works—not for any meritorious dignity which is, or can be, in the work, but through his mere mercy, and through whose commandment he works.

In contrast, the Roman doctrine is that just as pure water has no taste in and of itself, but takes on a pleasant smell if it passes through a pleasant smelling pipe, so our works gain neither satisfaction nor merit before we receive grace, but afterwards they gain both. Every such virtuous action, they thus maintain, has power to satisfy God's wrath against sin. They believe this to such an extent that if we commit no mortal sins or heinous crimes of our own on which to spend this treasure of satisfaction, it can secure the release of other men from Purgatory on whom the Pope is pleased to bestow it. Therefore, we may achieve satisfaction for the sin of both ourselves and others, but accrue merit only for

---

Tribulation (London: Charles Dolman, 1847), Chapter XII, pp. 39–40.

ourselves. In gaining merit, our actions work with two hands: with the one, they obtain their morning's stipend—that is, an increase of grace; with the other, they obtain their evening reward, the everlasting crown of glory. Indeed, Rome teaches that our good works achieve this not by originating from us, but by originating from grace in us. In their theology, this grace in us is something fundamentally different than what we mean when we speak of grace as the mere goodness of God's mercy toward us in Christ Jesus.

34. Would it be possible for them to see how plainly they contradict the very ground of apostolic faith if they were not possessed by a strong spirit of delusion? Is this the salvation by grace which the Scriptures speak of so frequently? Was this what was meant by those who first taught the world to look for salvation in Christ alone? "By grace," the Apostle says—and by grace in such a fashion as a gift, a thing that comes not of ourselves, not of our works, unless any man should boast and say, "I have wrought out my own salvation" (cf. Eph. 2:8–9; Phil. 2:12). The Church of Rome says says "by grace," but it is grace of such a sort, that any who wear the diadem of bliss in heaven would be wearing nothing other than what they have won themselves!

The Apostle, as if he had foreseen how the Church of Rome would later abuse the world by making "grace" such an ambiguous term in our salvation, says, "according to his mercy by which he saved us" (Titus 3:5). This mercy (although it does not exclude the washing of our new birth, the renewing of our hearts by the Holy Ghost, as well as the means, virtues, and duties which God requires from those who will be saved) is so incompatible with merit that to say that we are saved by the worthiness of anything which is ours is to deny that we are saved by grace. Grace gives freely, and therefore rightly demands that glory be ascribed only to that which is given. If we rest in the proud imagining that we deserve eternal life, that we merit it, and that we are worthy of it, then we deny the grace of our Lord Jesus Christ, debasing, annulling, annihilating the benefits of his bitter passion.

35. However, we must consider how many righteous men, saints, martyrs, and Church Fathers have had their various dangerous opinions. For example, some hoped to make amends for their sins by voluntarily punishing themselves, something which simply served to injure Christ. But shall we carve a deadly epitaph on their graves which says: "They directly denied the foundation of faith and are damned! There is no salvation for them"? St. Augustine once gave this counsel to himself: *Errare possum, haereticus esse nolo*.[15] Unless we draw a distinction between those who err, and those who obstinately persist in error, how could any man ever hope to be saved?

In this regard, I am no respecter of persons alive or dead! Show me a man of any status or condition whatsoever, yes, even a cardinal or a Pope, who in the final moments of his life has been brought to know himself by suffering, whose heart God has touched with true sorrow for all his sins, and filled with love for the Gospel of Christ, whose eyes are opened to see the truth, and whose mouth is opened to renounce all heresy and error of any kind, but

---

[15] "I can err, [but] I do not wish to be a heretic." This is a dubious quote found in this and other forms in the writings of Hooker and others from the late sixteenth century onwards. However, when this quote is searched for in *Patrologia Latina* no match is found. It is possible that this phrase was at some point falsely attributed to Augustine and henceforth assumed to be his. It may also be that this phrase is from a work no longer extant.

with one exception: this error regarding merits. He thinks God will require merit from him, and, because he lacks it, he trembles and feels discouraged, saying within himself, "Perhaps I myself am forgetful or unskilled, and not adequately 'furnished with things new and old' as a wise and learned scribe should be" (Mt. 13:52), and is unable to articulate that to which, if it were articulated, he would eagerly assent to, and thus be rescued from all his errors. But shall I think that, because of this single error, such a man cannot even hope to touch the hem of Christ's garment? If he does touch it, why should I not hope that virtue may proceed from Christ to save him? Shall I cast him off as one who has utterly cast off Christ, as one who does not hold on by so much as by a slender thread, because his error regarding merits overthrows his faith by logical consequence? No, I will not be afraid to say to a cardinal or to a Pope in this situation: "Be of good comfort. Ours is a merciful God who is ready to make the best of that little which we believe sincerely—not a clever sophist who finds the worst in all our errors."

Is there any reason that I should be thought suspect, or you that you should be offended, by such talk? Let us lay all emotion aside and let us consider the matter impartially: is it a dangerous thing to imagine that such men may find mercy? The hour may come when we shall think it a blessed thing to hear that, if our sins were like the sins of the Popes and cardinals, the depths of God's mercy are greater. I do not mean a Pope with the neck of an emperor under his foot, or a cardinal riding his horse bridle-deep in the blood of the saints; rather, a sorrowful and repentant Pope or cardinal—disrobed, stripped not only of usurped power, but also delivered and recalled from error and Antichrist, converted and lying prostrate at the feet of Christ. Can I think that Christ will spurn him? Can I oppose and contradict God's merciful promises which are made to all repentant sinners by excluding a Pope or a cardinal? What difference is there between a Pope and a cardinal and the man on the street in this case?

Let us imagine that, having once held their rank, it is impossible for a Pope or cardinal to be later touched with remorse. The Apostle says, "Though we, or an angel from heaven, should preach unto you," etc. (Gal. 1:8)—it seems as likely that St. Paul or an angel from heaven should preach heresy, as it does that a Pope or cardinal should come to acknowledge the truth! Yet if a Pope or a cardinal should do so, what exactly is it about them that would make us think they cannot be saved? "It is not about their persons," you might say, "but it is on account of the error that I suppose them to die—an error which excludes them from any hope of mercy." The opinion of merits supposedly removes all possibility of salvation from them.

But do you really think they are lost despite the fact that they only hold to merits as an error, while they hold the truth soundly and sincerely with regard to all the other doctrines of the Christian faith? Despite the fact that they have some measure of all the virtues and graces of the Spirit, and all other signs of God's elect children in them? Despite the fact that they are far from having any proud or presumptuous opinion that they deserve salvation for the worthiness of their deeds in and of themselves? Despite the fact that the only thing troubling and assaulting them is a little too much dejection, and an exaggerated fear arising from the mistaken idea that God requires a worthiness in them which they are grieved to find lacking? Despite the fact that they are not obstinate in this opinion? Despite the fact that they would gladly forsake this opinion, if just one sufficient reason could disprove it? Despite the fact that the only thing hindering them from forsaking this opinion before they die is ignorance of how it might be disproved, and this ignorance in turn the result of the ignorance of others who should be able to set them straight, but are not? Let me die if it ever should be proven that a simple error utterly excludes a Pope or a cardinal, in such a case, from the hope of life! I must confess: if it is an error to think that God may be merciful to save men even when they err, my greatest comfort is my error! If it were not for the love which I hold for this error, I would wish neither to speak nor to live!

VI:
CONCLUSION

36. IN VIEW of all the above then, I return to my opening thesis, which I had little thought would cause so much trouble: "I do not doubt that God was merciful to save thousands of our fathers living in popish superstitions, because they sinned ignorantly." Who knew what controversies were contained in this sentence that it should cause so much criticism! I said "Thousands of our fathers might be saved," and have demonstrated that it cannot be denied. I said "I do not doubt that they were saved," and I see no impiety in this conviction, even if I had no reason in the world for it. I said "Their ignorance makes me hope that they found mercy and so were saved"? What prevents salvation but sin? All sins are not equal; and although ignorance does not make sin cease to be sinful, if we agree that it made their sin less, why should it not make our hope concerning their life greater? We greatly pity those who sin due to lack of understanding, and I do not doubt that God has the greatest compassion for them. Other authors have made the same claim as mine, using much the same words. It is just my ill fortune that the same words, taken as true in other men's books, should seem to bolster heresy when recited by me. If I have been deceived on this point, it is not they, but the blessed Apostle

VI

who has deceived me! For what I have said of others, he said of himself, "I obtained mercy, because I did it ignorantly" (1 Tim. 1:13). If you understand his words, you cannot misunderstand mine! I speak nothing different, and I mean nothing different.

37. And so, at some length, I have brought the question of our fathers to an end. Having been offered the chance to do so, I considered it a valuable opportunity to offer my judgment so that all might see how wrong it is to say that we Protestants condemn all who came before us who did not share our own persuasions. This is especially important considering the weighty causes of separation between the Church of Rome and us, along with the weak arguments commonly used to keep men in the Roman Church (amongst which the example of our deceased fathers is one). Yet I did not desire to elaborate beyond that one sentence, judging it much more appropriate for us to regard our own state than to curiously sift over what has become of others; and fearing that such questions as these—if waded into too deeply—might seem worthy of the rebuke which our Savior thought needful in a similar case: "What is that to thee?" (Jn. 21:22). When I was unexpectedly forced to give an account of my words, I had to rise to the challenge, as others called on me to do, proceeding as duty dictated to offer fuller satisfaction of men's minds. To that end, I have chosen to act with reverence and with fear: with reverence for our fathers who lived in former times; and not without fear, for those who are alive.

38. I am not ignorant as to how ready men are to feed and to soothe themselves with evil. "Shall I," says the man who loves the present world more than he loves Christ (cf. 2 Tim. 4:10), "incur the high displeasure of the mightiest

upon earth? Shall I risk my goods, endanger my position, and jeopardize my life, rather than yield to that which so many of my fathers have embraced, and yet found favor in the sight of God?" "Curse ye Meroz," says the Lord, "curse ye bitterly the inhabitant thereof, because they came not to the help of Jehovah, to the help of Jehovah against the mighty" (Judg. 5:23). If I should not only fail to help the Lord against the mighty, but also help to strengthen the mighty against the Lord, I might deservedly fall under the burden of that curse, and be worthy of judgment. But if the doctrine which I teach is a flower gathered in the garden of the Lord, a part of the saving truth of the Gospel, from which poisoned creatures still manage to suck venom, I can only wish that it were otherwise. I must be content with my lot, and all the more so because it has not befallen me alone. St. Paul preached truth, and a consoling truth at that, when he taught that the greater our misery regarding our iniquities, all the more ready is the mercy of our God for our release if we seek him. The more we have sinned, the more praise, and glory and honor that goes to him who pardons our sin!

But note what perverse interpretations some made of this. The Apostle says: "Why am I also still judged as a sinner? And why not (as we are slanderously reported, and as some affirm that we say), let us do evil, that good may come?" (Rom. 3:7–8). He was accused of teaching that which malicious men drew from his teaching, even though it was clearly not only different from his teaching, but against its very meaning. The Apostle adds, "Their condemnation who do thus is just." As for me, I am not hasty to apply sentences of condemnation to anyone. I wish from my heart for the conversion of anyone so perversely wrong, since anyone who hardens themselves, presuming upon God's mercy toward others, is in a fearful and dangerous state.

It is true that God is merciful, but let us beware of presumptuous sins (Ps. 19:13). Yes, God delivered Jonah from the bottom of the sea, but will any of you therefore cast yourselves headlong from the tops of rocks and say in your hearts, "God shall deliver us" (cf. Mt. 4:5–7)? Yes, he pities the blind that would gladly see, but will God pity him who can see and yet hardens himself in blindness? No, Christ has spoken too much to you for you to claim the privilege of your fathers.

39. Whether in regard to this matter or any other, those of us who have considered the case of our fathers should consider the good counsel which the Wise Man gives: "Stand thou fast in thy sure understanding, in the way and knowledge of the Lord, and have but one manner of word, and follow the word of peace and righteousness" (Ecclesiasticus 5:10). As a loose tooth is a great grief to one who eats, so is a doubtful and uncertain word an offense in speech that seeks to instruct. "Should a wise man answer with vain knowledge, and fil himself with the east wind?" says Eliphaz—light, inconstant, unstable words? (Job 15:2). Even the wisest may speak words of the wind; the fallen state of our nature is such that we neither perfectly understand the ways and knowledge of the Lord, nor do we perfectly embrace it when it is understood, nor graciously speak it when it is embraced, nor peacefully maintain it when it is spoken. But even the best of us are sometimes overtaken with blindness, sometimes with hastiness, sometimes with impatience, and sometimes with other passions of the mind, to which God knows that we are also subjected.

Therefore, we must be content both to pardon others, and to desire that others may pardon us for such things. No one, while they live, should think of themselves as always free from errors and oversights in their speech. I hope that the things which I have said to you are sound, although they will have seemed otherwise to some. If I have been insulted by them over all this, I willingly forget it. But truthfully, considering the benefit which I have reaped from this necessary search for truth, I prefer the assertion of the Apostle: "Ye did me no wrong" (Gal. 4:12). I sincerely wish them as many blessings in the kingdom of heaven as they have forced me to utter words and syllables on this matter, in which I could not have been more sparing in speech than I have been. St. Jerome says, "It befits no man to be patient with regard to the crime of heresy" (*To Pammachius, against John of Jerusalem*, ca. 409).[1]

I take it that we should always be patient, even if the crime of heresy was intended. However, beloved, I could not, I dared not, be silent in a matter of such great consequence as this—especially since my love for the truth in Christ Jesus had been somewhat called into question. Therefore, in the meekness of Christ (2 Cor. 10:1), I urge those that had first made an issue out of this, to consider how a watchman may cry, "An enemy!" when, in fact, a friend is coming. In such a case, I deem a watchman more deserving of love for his carefulness than of dislike for his mistake;

---

[1] Jerome, *Contra Joannem Hierosolymitanum, ad Pammachium, liber unus*, 2 (PL 23:0357A). Jerome (c. 342–420) was one of the great Church Fathers, most known for his Latin translation of the Bible. He wrote *To Pammachius, against John of Jerusalem* (cited here) in the midst of the First Origenist Controversy, in which Jerome and others pressured John II, the Bishop of Jerusalem (c. 356–417), to posthumously condemn Origen (c. 184–253) as a heretic.

VI

and so I have determined, as much as it lies with me in this case, to take away any suspicion of unfriendly intent or purpose against the truth, from which, God knows, my heart is free.

40. Now to you, beloved, who have heard these things, I will use no other words of admonition than those which are offered to me by St. James: "My brethren, hold not the faith of our Lord Jesus Christ, the Lord of glory, in respect of persons" (James 2:1). You are now to learn that, just as there is no harm in hearing the different judgments of men in questionable cases, nor should it be scandalous and offensive to anyone. Cephas may have one interpretation, and Apollos another; Paul may be of this mind, and Barnabas of that. If this offends you, the fault is yours. Maintain peaceful minds and you might find comfort in this diversity.

Now may the God of peace give you peaceful minds, and use them to your everlasting comfort!

WANT TO SUGGEST IMPROVEMENTS?

Given our desire to build on what we have begun here and to make this work as truthful, faithful, and useful as possible, we invite corrections and suggested improvements from all our readers (be they as small as a typo or as large as suggesting a different rendering of a key passage). If you desire to submit such a suggestion or correction, please email it to editor@davenantinstitute.org and we will take it under consideration for inclusion in a later revised edition.

ABOUT THE LIBRARY OF EARLY ENGLISH PROTESTANTISM

The Library of Early English Protestantism (LEEP) is a multi-year project that aims to make available in scholarly but accessible editions seminal writings from key but neglected sixteenth- and seventeenth-century Church of England theologians. This project intends to bring old resources to a new audience, specifically for those Reformed and Anglican readers seeking to deepen and broaden their understanding of their theological tradition. The purpose of LEEP is to make the rediscovery of these sources as easy as possible by providing affordable, comprehensively-edited, modernized-spelling editions for contemporary seminarians, clergy, students, and theologically-concerned laypeople.

In this series:

James Ussher and the Reformed Episcopal Church: Sermons and Treatises on Ecclesiology, edited by Dr. Richard Snoddy (2018).

Apology of the Church of England by John Jewel, edited by Andre Gazal (2020).

Jurisdiction Regal, Episcopal, Papal by George Carleton, edited by Andre Gazal (2021).

ABOUT THE DAVENANT INSTITUTE

The Davenant Institute aims to retrieve the riches of classical Protestantism in order to renew and build up the contemporary church: building networks of friendship and collaboration among evangelical scholars committed to Protestant resourcement, publishing resources old and new, and offering training and discipleship for Christians thirsting after wisdom.

We are a nonprofit organization supported by your tax-deductible gifts. Learn more about us, and donate, at www.davenantinstitute.org.